T0305018

Baby-Led Weaning
Made Easy

Baby-Led Weaning Made Easy

Includes 70 nutritious weaning
recipes for 6 to 18+ months

Sian Radford

Contents

Dear Reader,

Starting your baby on solid foods is a special moment; it's the beginning of what we hope will be for them a healthy lifetime relationship with, and love of, good food. Weaning is a word that I feel barely does justice to this process; I prefer to call it an introduction to the wonderful world of food. It's a very important window during which you can offer your baby a wide variety of tastes, textures, colours and flavours that can positively influence their food preferences for years to come. Yes, it can be daunting, but as Sian shows it can also be wonderful journey shared by parent and baby.

I have worked in child, adolescent and infant nutrition for around 20 years, and there is a lot of information out there. But when it comes to food and nutrition, it's important not to get bogged down with different theories and methods. The best advice is to keep it simple by preparing and enjoying tasty, nutritious meals. And that applies to both you and your baby. Whether baby-led weaning (giving finger foods) or spoon-feeding, there is no either/or, but a combination of both gives baby the best of both worlds. Sian presents her method of starting solids with baby in a fresh and imaginative way; her recipes are tasty and nutritious, and they provide an introduction to the different tastes, flavours, textures and colours that I mentioned. Sian's informative and inspiring approach shows how you can ensure this time is special and enjoyable both for baby and you.

You may have lots of questions at this milestone, but so much of this process is intuitive. No one knows your baby better than you, and they will determine when they want to eat, how much, and which foods. Your job is to offer the food – they will decide how much of it they want to eat. This is baby's first opportunity to express choice (and they will!), however, if they refuse a food, keep trying – baby doesn't know what they like yet, and studies have shown that it can take up to 20 exposures to a new food before a baby will accept it.

Also, don't compare your baby with other babies. Lovely Rue, whose experiences of her introduction to food led to Sian sharing her progress and became the inspiration for this book, has a brilliant relationship with food, but it is of course a story of ebbs and flows and likes and dislikes along the way. Don't put yourself under any pressure is the overarching message. If you feel that your baby isn't quite ready for certain foods or textures, try something else and wait until you feel they are ready. This is part of their journey in creating their own positive relationship with food.

Three things I'd like to mention that sum up the heart of the book:

1. Offer home-cooked food and avoid the processed foods in jars and pouches. Remember that from 6 months baby can eat what you eat, as long as you don't add salt and chilli and you keep the food soft and moist.

2. Limit sugar – let baby derive sweetness from naturally sweet foods, such as fruit.

3. Go easy on yourself – there's enough guilt that comes with parenting without including food. Enjoy this time.

Food is both pleasure and function. Keep it fun, sociable and interactive. Keep stress away from the dinner table and make mealtimes a time of family interaction, fun and love. Enjoy the book!

Yinka Thomas MSc RNutr.

Introduction

Hello!

I'm Sian (pronounced cyan, like the colour) – the mum, content creator and cook behind TikTok's @moonandrue.

Before we dive into this world of weaning, feeding tips and baby- and toddler-friendly recipes, I want to share a secret with you... I don't think I'm a particularly amazing cook. I don't come from a long line of great family cooks – sorry, Mum – and I don't feel like cooking is my happy place in the way that some others do (eating might be, but that's a different story!).

That might seem like an odd way to welcome you to this book, but I think it's important to set that straight, because when it comes to weaning (and cooking for your family in general), you don't need to follow lengthy recipes that require lots of skill. You don't have to spend hours in the kitchen. You don't need to be an expert.

Weaning does not have to be complicated. A weaning diet is like any other: it has some rules, certain foods you should prioritise and other foods you're better off avoiding. But once you've learnt those – and I will share everything you need to know in the first section of this book – you can create simple, wholesome, nutritious meals that give your baby everything they need in order to grow and develop.

I started documenting my daughter's weaning journey on TikTok in May 2022, sharing two of her meals each week alongside recipes and general tips and advice. It has been the biggest privilege to have so many other parents use my recipes and advice in their own weaning journeys, and to know that we've helped people feel more confident and less overwhelmed about the process.

I want this book to spread those feelings far and wide. It's got all of my best tips, recipes and must-knows in one place. Picture it like a big sister, holding your hand and guiding you through the process.

These are just some of the things you'll know after reading this book:

- ☑ What your baby should eat and when.

- ☑ What behaviours to expect and when they might happen.

- ☑ How to introduce allergens safely.

- ☑ How to encourage and develop key skills, like using cutlery.

- ☑ Techniques for handling fussy eating.

- ☑ Great recipes for all ages from 6 months to 2 years (and beyond!).

I hope this book is a great companion to your weaning adventure. There is nothing better than seeing babies enjoying their food and knowing that you're giving them the best possible start!

Sian

Crash Course

This first section of the book will take you on a tour of all the information you need to know to ensure you are prepped and ready for getting started with weaning.

Why baby-led weaning?

Methods of weaning and preferences on how to approach it will differ depending on a person's family dynamic, culture, the support they have at home, flexibility of their daily timetable and what they're comfortable with. I can't stress enough that you have to do what works for you and your family. The only caveat to this is that, with weaning, it's developmental. So, if you're hesitant, or delay progress, or don't introduce allergens in optimal windows of time, there can potentially be negative impacts for your child further down the line. At 6 months they are ready for textured food, so although there is nothing wrong with starting your baby on purées, this must be done in the knowledge that you progress through chunkier textures and on to finger foods, ideally by 9 months. Baby-led weaning, the method we used with Rue, incorporates finger foods in a safe way from the very start. As long as your baby is around 6 months and is showing the three signs of readiness (I'll talk more about this in an upcoming section), then baby-led weaning is a fantastic option. Let me explain why I love it so much:

1 **It teaches the key skills of eating.** This might sound like I'm kicking things off with Captain Obvious but, simply put, baby-led weaning allows your little one to properly experience foods in their true forms. Spoon feeding will give your baby exposure to tastes and fill their bellies, but baby-led weaning gives exposure to tastes, real food textures in the hand and mouth, and builds their chewing and swallowing skills. With baby-led weaning, the 'filling the bellies' bit can come a little later compared to spoon feeding, as it can seem like not much is swallowed at first, but at this point your baby is still on all of their milk feeds and therefore it isn't as essential for them to eat full meals in the early stages. What is essential, though, is aiming to provide them with key nutrients (you can find out more about this on page 22).

2 **It encourages intuitive eating.** From day one, Rue decided what she was eating first on her plate and when she'd had enough. It's harder to achieve this with spoon feeding as, naturally, it's more parent-led and us adults are conditioned to want to see an empty bowl! I feel like baby-led weaning has allowed Rue to establish foundations for a healthy relationship with food. Having everything on her plate at once means she's not classifying foods as 'good', 'bad' or 'rewards'. I decide on her diet, I offer the food, but it's her who takes authority over everything else. She eats until she's satisfied and learns to listen to her body for those cues, rather than having food delivered to her mouth and not having as much reason to tune into those aspects.

3 **It develops motor skills.** This one was a key selling point for me. In my former life I was a teacher, both in primary and secondary schools. In every class I taught, from age 5 to age 19, there would always be a chunk of students who struggled to access the learning because of their difficulties with fine motor skills. Handwriting, glueing work into their books, using a ruler or scissors, typing – even skills like tying shoes. The physical demand for children with poorly developed motor skills is huge, and it spills over into mental demand in trying to keep up with everything else. School obviously isn't the be-all and end-all – I am purely using that as an example of how struggling with motor skills can spill out into so many areas of everyday living – and, of course, baby-led weaning isn't the one and only solution to developing motor skills, and a lack of baby-led weaning isn't a root cause of those issues either, but being able to give Rue quality daily opportunities to develop these skills and have sensory messy play at the same time made this sort of weaning a really attractive option.

Do they eat the same as us?

I had my heart set on baby-led weaning before Rue had even arrived. I'd heard anecdotes of how seamlessly it can fit into everyday life, with baby eating the same meals as the rest of the family. I had romantic visions of Rue joining us at dinnertime, tucking into a salmon stir-fry and a glass of red...

You won't be surprised to hear that my vision has yet to become a reality. I was naive. The fact of the matter is, a baby's dietary needs are simply different to those of an adult. The way foods are served needs to be adjusted for maximum safety, they have specific nutritional needs and, to top it all off, babies have their dinner at a time that can only be described, at best, as late afternoon. So the idea that they eat the same as us doesn't always work out.

The good news is, a lot of meals only need minor tweaks to make them suitable for the whole family. Where that's not possible, building a freezer stash of quick options for your baby is key to keeping your sanity and ensuring everyone's needs are met. I find this particularly handy at lunchtime, which, as an adult, is a meal I tend to overlook. 'Fail to prepare, prepare to fail' and all that. It's like I don't see lunch coming, then all of a sudden I'm ravenous, so I end up throwing together a salad at the last minute. And by salad I mean cheese toastie with a bag of crisps... On those days, I am always thankful for my freezer stash of iron-rich, nutritious foods that I can give to Rue with minimal time and effort.

So how should you tweak meals to make sure they work for everyone? There are some key differences between adults and babies when it comes to nutrition, which you need to consider when cooking and portioning out meals:

FOOD	WHY?	TIPS
Sugar	We're talking added sugars. Yes, there are naturally occurring sugars in a lot of foods, and while it's good to be mindful of them, they're not the issue here. Tooth decay, obesity, high blood pressure, heart disease and type 2 diabetes are just some of the things we're keeping at bay when we keep our little ones away from the sweet stuff.	Avoid sweeteners like honey*, maple syrup, jams, fruit juice, fruit yoghurts and sauces like ketchup. *Honey should never be given to under-1s – see further down the table for more info.
Salt	Again, we're talking added salts. Sodium is also naturally occurring in foods and is actually essential to the human body in small amounts. However, adding salt to baby's food is a big no-no. Until the age of 1, their kidneys simply aren't developed enough to process it. Eating too much salt can also negatively impact the body's ability to absorb calcium, which is a key nutrient for their growth and bone health. After 1 you can relax the reins a little, but it's still advisable to be mindful of how much is added throughout the day. Salt intake guidelines: Under 1 – less than 1g per day 1–3 years – no more than 2g per day 4–6 years – no more than 3g per day 7–10 years – no more than 5g per day	Avoid stock cubes, gravy, bacon, sausages, ham, some breads and salty cheeses like feta, halloumi, Parmesan and mature Cheddar. Look for very low-salt stock varieties, containing 0.1g salt per 100g (if you're in the UK, Piccolo or Kallo brand offer these). Cook the whole family meal with no salt/stock cubes and add salt to your plate, or a small amount of low-salt stock cubes. You can also separate out your baby's portions to keep it salt-free.

Remember, your little one thus far has survived on a diet of milk, milk and more milk. What seems bland to us is actually very flavourful for them. When it comes to salt and sugar, you can be sure that your baby will eventually discover (and like) both, with no interference needed from you. Sugar and salt have corrupted adult taste buds so intensely that it's hard to find a commercial product on the shelves that does not contain one or both. And once you set the sugar and salt wheels in motion, taste buds tend to demand more and more of them. So, for now, know that you're doing your baby a great service in giving their little body time to grow without interference from either.

FOOD	WHY?	TIPS
Allergens	For at least the first month of weaning, you will want to take caution around allergens that you are exposing your baby to, and watch for any potential reactions as they try them. You can find my advice for introducing allergens on page 42. Allergenic foods to watch out for are gluten (wheat, barley and rye), eggs, cow's milk and dairy, fish, tree nuts, peanuts, soya, sesame, seeds such as mustard and poppy seeds, celery and shellfish.	Introduce one allergen food at a time (for example, some hard-boiled egg served with a non-allergen food), before offering multiple allergen foods as part of a meal (for example, cheese omelette with buttered toast, which uses dairy, egg and wheat).

FOOD	WHY?	TIPS
Low-Fat	This is an example where the advice for adults is pretty much the opposite of what's needed for a baby. Where we are advised to reduce our intake of saturated fats, babies need it for rapid growth. They also need omega 3 fats for brain development. If you're hoping to share your dairy products with your baby, ditch the low-fat options. The good news is there are emerging studies that suggest full-fat dairy products can actually have a positive impact on heart health for adults, which means these options can work quite well for all the family.	Full-fat milk, cheese and yoghurts are the best options as they are calorie- and nutrient-dense and packed with the fats needed to support rapid growth.
Iron	This nutrient is so important to weaning that I've actually included an entire section on it starting on page 25. The TLDR version? Iron is a nutrient that needs to take high priority in a weaning baby's diet. The good news? It's a nutrient that babies, children and adults alike are most likely to be deficient in, meaning incorporating more is a win-win for everyone. The bad news? It's a nutrient that babies, children and adults alike are most likely to be deficient in. . . suggesting that most of us aren't actually very good at eating enough of it! It's important to be deliberate and intentional in making sure that your baby's meals contain iron-rich foods; luckily, this is much easier than it sounds, and I've included tonnes of ideas throughout this book to help you do just that.	Include iron-rich foods throughout your baby's meals. You can find a list of iron-rich foods on page 26, and many of the recipes in this book are rich in iron!
Honey	Not only is honey a sugar, it can also contain a nasty bacteria that causes an illness called botulism. Infant botulism can be fatal, so it's advised to avoid honey with your little ones until they are one. From the age of one, the human body has developed enough immunity to combat the nasty bacteria, so it's no longer a threat, although honey would remain a very sugary option, so continue to bear that in mind.	There is a misguided belief that cooking honey removes the threat of botulism, however, the World Health Organization (WHO) states that this can only be done in a highly pressurised heated environment and cannot be achieved by home cooking appliances.

FOOD	WHY?	TIPS
Wholegrains	Wholegrains (such as brown rice, wholegrain breads and wholewheat pasta) are nutritious powerhouses, full of vitamins and fibre, which are great for helping us grown-ups to feel fuller for longer. However, when it comes to babies, high-fibre foods can result in them becoming full very quickly, and as a result not eating the variety of other nutrients that they need. Moderation is key here – always serve wholegrains and their refined counterparts as part of a varied diet. Be mindful of portion sizes, too, as wholegrains will be more filling. As always with babies, keep an eye on any changes in the nappy department, because too much fibre can cause constipation (or diarrhoea. . . just to keep you on your toes).	For a 6-month-old, 1 or 2 portions of wholegrains per day is more than enough. For a 9- to 12-month-old, this can be gradually increased to 2 to 4 portions. A portion could be a toasted soldier, half a Weetabix, or a tablespoon of porridge oats.
Seasoning	Spices are safe from 6 months old, and how you choose to introduce them really comes down to personal, familial and cultural preferences. Babies around the world will be exposed to a variety of flavours and heat levels in their foods, however, it is generally advised to leave 'hotter' spices until at least 9–12 months, as they can irritate the digestive tract and lining of the stomach. Introduce them gently and gradually in order to allow time for your baby to get familiar with the sensations, and keep an eye out for any digestive consequences like tummy pain or poo changes. Personally, I left 'first tastes' of foods plain to allow Rue to get to know the food in its actual form. I then introduced subtle spices like smoked paprika, cumin, cinnamon, mild and then medium curry powder, garlic and onion powders.	Bear in mind that most pre-packaged seasoning mixes will contain too much salt for a baby, so it's best to avoid these until they are at least one. Stick to jars that simply contain the individual spice.

What you actually need

Starting weaning can feel like an overwhelming task. On top of that, we've also got to deal with technology constantly spying on us. If you so much as think about the word 'weaning', your social media feed will immediately be bombarded with every brand, product and gadget out there. My advice would be to keep things simple. Once weaning is underway you'll have a better idea of what your baby needs and what products suit their approach.

I spent an embarrassing amount on cute plates in the lead up to weaning. I'll admit it became a bit of an obsession, but the designs were adorable and I justified it all to myself because Rue was going to get so much use out of them! Fast-forward a month or so into weaning and I was both humbled and distraught to discover that my daughter's favourite game was plate-flipping. Every mealtime she was hellbent in sending my lovely (but non-suction and therefore useless) plates tumbling to the floor whenever she got the opportunity. It took a lot to swallow my pride, pack away my failed plate collection and get online to buy more – this time with suction pads! Cover your basics, but know that you don't need absolutely every item in order to get started. And definitely don't get carried away buying cute plates. Ahem…

For Mealtimes:

The following essentials will keep mealtimes running smoothly and offer some much-needed damage control for any mess!

A highchair with footrest

Options on the market are endless, but we kept things simple with the IKEA Antilop highchair and a footrest from Etsy. It's inexpensive and we love that we can adjust the footrest as Rue grows. It's meant she has been able to use the footrest correctly throughout weaning. If you have a chair with a fixed footrest, stacking some books on it to close the gap up to baby's foot height can be a solution. While many highchair models do not have a footrest at all, I would recommend getting one that does (or has the option for one to be added, such as in the IKEA chair). One scenario that really helped me visualise and understand this was to imagine I was doing a skill that was alien to me – such as writing on an easel with my non-dominant hand – then imagine how much harder this would be if I were sat on a bar stool with my legs dangling down and no firm surface there for core support. In the same way, the footrest helps provide a stable base to allow your baby to focus on the other physical skills they are concentrating on, and being comfortable and supported will help with their stamina at mealtimes too.

Your baby should have a straight back in the chair, with their ankles, knees and hips at a 90-degree angle. This provides the best foundations for swallowing safely and reaching and grasping foods easily.

Plates and bowls

Some people like to serve food directly on the highchair table, but I always found it best to try to emulate a proper mealtime as much as possible. Suction plates and bowls are great if you have a plate-flipper like Rue! Most popular plates are either bamboo or silicone; each have their own benefits. Bamboo naturally has antibacterial properties, and these plates tend to have the best suction, but they shouldn't be put in the dishwasher or microwave, as heat will cause the wood to swell. Silicone is microwave-, freezer- and dishwasher-safe, however, I find that handwashing with mild dish soap is still the best option, as silicone can take on food tastes and smells over time, and regular dishwashing causes this to worsen. Open plates are great in the early days, as dividers can be tricky to navigate for tiny arms and hands, but there are lots of styles to choose from! You can definitely survive with just one plate and one bowl if you don't mind the regular washing up.

Cups

It's advised that you should give your baby sips of water alongside their solid meals. Weaning is a great time to let your baby learn how to drink from an open cup and a straw cup – I liked to use both on rotation as they are separate skills, which will be carried into childhood and adult life. Now that Rue is a little older and she drinks water outside of mealtimes too, we use open cups during meals and straw cups around the house. Sippy cups with valves are not recommended as they have been linked to negative impacts on speech and language development and oral health, but free-flow beakers, open cups and straw cups are all fine.

Cutlery

One suggested 'downside' of baby-led weaning is that it can delay cutlery use. There is absolutely nothing wrong with your baby eating with their hands, but it doesn't hurt to be intentional about having cutlery present at mealtimes. Even if in the early days it's just there for your baby to mouth on and then throw on the floor 95 per cent of the time!

There are a variety of pre-spoons available that are designed to pick up soft foods such as yoghurt with a dipping – rather than a scooping – action. There are also cutlery sets with ergonomic handles, and of course regular silicone or plastic cutlery sets. There's no need to overdo it, but having some cutlery present during mealtimes, pre-loading a few mouthfuls and handing it to them, will allow your baby to build the links and start their journey to using it independently.

Bibs

This one is primarily for your own sanity. I always found it helpful to have an apron/smock-style bib, with a silicone catch-all bib over the top. The apron bibs protect their clothes and often catch extra in the lap, so that there is less mess on the floor. The silicone bib catches any missed mouthfuls and you can scoop it back onto their plate or (even better) your baby will discover the joys of bib diving and go digging for their missing food themselves!

There are obvious culprits for staining – tomato-based sauces, recipes containing colourful spices such as turmeric or paprika – but beyond that there are also many textures, such as banana, which are surprisingly difficult to get out of fabrics. So, all in all, the cover-ups are your best bet to saving clothes and reducing laundry.

Soft microfibre cloths

Another clean-up essential. I bought a few packs of microfibre cloths in particular colours that are specifically just for clearing up after Rue's meals. Buy enough to have them on laundry rotation and use them to wipe your baby's hands and face before the cover-alls come off. They are better for the planet than wipes and they will stay separate from any cloths you use for cleaning.

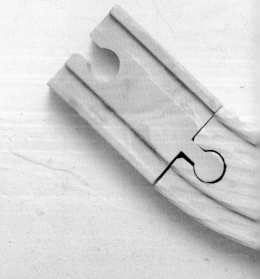

For the kitchen:

Below are my most-used items to make all the extra food prep easier and quicker; I highly recommend you have these in your kitchen.

Food storage

With weaning, batch cooking is your best friend. Stock up on freezer bags and Tupperware to ensure you've got everything you need to freeze meals in portions and save as much food as possible. Freezer bags, which can be bought in food-safe plastic or more sustainable silicone, are a personal favourite as they take up so much less space than tubs. Squeeze any air out of the bag before closing it, then they can be frozen flat – a great space-saver if you don't have much room in the freezer. I also like using food cube trays (sort of like large ice cube trays) for sauces, jams and purées.

A blender

Even with baby-led weaning, there will be plenty of times you'll want to whizz something up to a smoother texture, or make a batter or purée. Any blender will do, but I did find my hand blender particularly useful, as you can use it so quickly without having to transfer food into different containers.

Microwave

Okay, you probably already have one, but I just wanted to take a moment because I don't know what I would do without my microwave when it comes to weaning. I use the defrost settings for batch-cooked frozen meals when I've forgotten to take them out in time. I use it to steam vegetables, as this retains more nutrients than pan methods of steaming or boiling. I use it to cook meals such as porridge with much more ease than on the hob. One thing to be careful of when microwaving is hot spots, as the food can heat inconsistently and leave some areas piping hot. Regular stirring between cooking intervals can help eliminate this, and obviously it's important to thoroughly stir and check the food before you give it to your little one. I test the temperature of foods by touching them to my lip before serving it to Rue. Lips are 100 times more sensitive than fingertips, so you'll soon know if it's too hot for your baby!

Signs of readiness

Weaning is (and should be!) a hugely exciting time. You might
be raring to go, counting down the seconds until the clock chimes
and you can offer those first tastes. But there are a few key things to
look out for before you get started. You will likely hear lots of stories
of people weaning much earlier or later than the recommended
6 months, but remember, it's not about other people's expectations,
or even your own excitement (sorry), it's about knowing your baby
is ready to begin solids safely.

One of the reasons weaning begins at around 6 months old is because
this is when a baby's iron stores from being in the womb begin to
deplete. But the truth is, readiness for weaning is not something
that magically happens overnight on the date they turn that age. It's
more a state of being than an age, so it's all about looking out for the
developmental cues that your little one is ready. Some babies might
display these behaviours by the time they're 6 months, some may
need to wait a few weeks more. If your baby is older than 6 months and
you still feel you're worried about your baby's progress with the three
skills opposite, reach out to your doctor or health visitor for some
guidance and support.

SKILL	WHAT TO LOOK FOR	WAYS TO PRACTISE
Bringing food to their own mouth Why? So your baby can access their meals independently and self-feed with success.	Can your baby grasp objects – whether that's from the table or something you've handed to them – and use their hand-eye coordination to lift it to their mouth?	Teething toys! Especially ones that have longer sections. Not only does this give them practice with bringing things to their mouth and improving their eye, hand and mouth coordination, but longer teething toys also introduce them to the back sections of their mouth and their gag reflex.
Independent sitting Why? A crucial skill to ensure that your baby has the stability to swallow solids safely and reduce the risk of choking.	Can your baby sit upright in their highchair with a stable neck and torso, without help from a parent?	Sitting practice! In your lap, surrounded by cushions on the floor or in a sit-me-up-style ring or chair. Tummy time will also encourage the muscle development needed for trunk stability. In a highchair, there will be a little leaning in the early days, but they should have the core strength to keep themselves from folding forwards or slouching down.
Loss of tongue-thrust reflex Why? The loss of this primitive reflex shows your baby's brain has developed enough to respond to swallowing solid foods.	Can you touch your baby's lips and/or tongue without their tongue reflexively sticking out in response?	This reflex is mostly present from 4–6 months, then it gradually reduces. It is best to wait for your baby to lose this reflex naturally. There are things that support the loss of tongue thrust, such as introducing a straw cup or discontinuing the use of a dummy, but for the most part these ideas are reserved for babies approaching 7 months who still have not lost the reflex.

Nutrients 101

There's an endless amount to know about food, but when you've got a baby, having the time to learn it all is not a luxury you have! The likelihood is, when it comes to nutrients you want to know:

1 Their role in your baby's health and development.

2 How much of each one your baby needs each day.

3 The best foods you can offer that will get the job done.

So, in the spirit of keeping things brief, here is that info! As with all things food, don't worry about being too prescriptive. There are certainly foods to prioritise over others, but aim to include wholesome, nutritious ingredients as much as possible and you can't go far wrong.

Carbohydrates

Carbs are made up of starches and sugars, and carbohydrate foods contain a mixture of starch and sugar in different proportions. They provide the body with energy – something your baby needs a lot of for all of the growing that's going on! They also aid healthy digestion and sleep.

Starches

These can be unrefined (such as wholegrain bread, cereal, beans, potatoes, sweet potatoes) or refined (white bread, pasta, flour, etc). Unrefined starches offer slow-release energy whereas refined starches are quick-release and not as nutritious. It's still important to strike a balance between wholegrain and refined options with your baby, because wholegrains are fibrous and it's advised to avoid a high-fibre diet with children under 5. Aim to give a mix of wholegrain and refined starches while your little one is under 2 – you can then gradually introduce them over time after this age.

1 portion = roughly the size of your baby's clenched fist
Aim to offer 5 portions a day (a minimum of 4)

UNREFINED	REFINED
Wholegrain bread	White bread
Brown rice	White rice
Oats	White pasta
Beans	Flour
Potatoes	Pizza dough
Sweet potatoes	Processed breakfast
Lentils	cereals

Sugars

There are many different types of naturally occurring sugars that are fine in a baby's diet, such as lactose, which you find in milk. Fruit and vegetables also contain natural sugars. These sugars are attached to the plant cells and fibre, which means the sugar is absorbed at a gradual rate and is less likely to damage the teeth. Also, fruit and vegetables are high in other nutrients, which makes them overall far more beneficial than other sugar sources.

For fruit and vegetables:

> 1 portion = a serving the size of your baby's cupped hand
>
> Aim to offer 5 portions a day (aim for more vegetables than fruit overall)

Your baby does not need any added sugar beyond what is present in natural, whole foods.

Free sugars

Whenever you cook fruits, such as steaming, stewing, or to purée them, you are breaking down the cells of the plant and therefore turning some of the sugars inside into what's known as 'free sugars'. Free sugars are like the feral child at soft play who is seemingly unsupervised, running around causing absolute carnage with no responsible adult in sight. They are empty calories, so they hold little nutritional benefit, and they are highly damaging to teeth.

In commercially produced purées especially, the fruits are exposed to high-pressure cooking environments, which can result in a large amount of the fruit fibre being broken down (compared to what you could manage with your equipment at home). This is why, from a sugar's perspective, the best way to offer fruits is in their purest form. The next best thing would be home-cooked or puréed fruits. Dried fruits also contain higher amounts of sugar, so it is best to offer them in moderation.

Free sugars to avoid include:

- Table sugar
- Maple syrup
- Honey (which should never be given to under-1s due to the risk of botulism)
- Fruit yoghurts
- Fruit juices, smoothies and concentrates
- Squash

Many commercial baby snacks sold today unfortunately contain high amounts of fruit concentrate. When reading a nutritional label, look for the amount of sugar per 100g to get an idea of what percentage of that snack is sugar.

> **Note from a nutritionist:** Beware of 'No added sugar*' – You might pick up a product like baby porridge and feel reassured that it's labelled 'no added sugar*'. However, on closer inspection, the label will say that the same product contains between 26 and 31 per cent sugar, depending on the brand. So how is this the case? That's where the asterisk comes in. Manufacturers can state 'contains only naturally occurring sugars', which allows them to claim there is no added sugar, but these 'naturally occurring sugars' are free sugars, and depending on how much is used, they can give food the same level of sweetness as table sugar. Giving these products as baby's first foods can condition them to crave sweetness. So don't be fooled by the asterisk, instead give baby plain porridge oats sweetened with soft fruits like banana or berries.

Fats

As the most energy-dense nutrient, fat is key to brain development and healthy brain function. There are also many vitamins that are fat-soluble, meaning your baby needs to eat fats in order for these vitamins to actually be absorbed by the body.

Healthy fats come in the form of both unsaturated and saturated fats, and many foods contain a mixture of both types of fat.

Healthy sources of unsaturated fats	Healthy sources of saturated fats

Olive oil
Avocados
Seeds
Nuts
Nut butters
Salmon
Sardines
	Coconut oil
	Cheese
	Butter (unsalted for
	  babies)
	Eggs
	Full-fat milk and
	  yoghurt
	Fats in unprocessed
	  meat (in moderation)

High-fat meals are a good thing for your baby; as they only eat a small amount but are growing at a rapid pace, they need their meals to be rich in energy, and fats provide an abundance of that.

1 portion = When it comes to fats, it's hard to give guidance on portion sizes as it varies depending on the food source (a quarter of an avocado would be lovely, but that same amount in pure butter does not make much sense!). Simply aim to include a range of healthy fats across your little one's meals, stick to full-fat dairy products where possible and don't restrict their fat sources.

Note from a nutritionist: Fats – It's important that your baby gets a supply of omega 3 fats in their diet because they're vital for both brain development and brain function. The best sources are oily fish – sardines, salmon, mackerel, anchovies and herring (kippers). Obviously, anchovies and kippers are too salty for baby, and mackerel can be quite salty when it's sold pre-cooked in packs, so sardines and salmon are the best choices, also because of their soft texture. Try to give baby at least one portion of sardines or salmon a week, if possible. Sardines would be my favoured choice, because while oily fish can contain low levels of chemical pollutants that can build up in the body, sardines have very low levels of these as they are much lower in the food chain. Government advice is that boys should have no more than 4 portions of oily fish a week, and girls no more than 2 portions a week.

Protein

Protein is made up of a chain of amino acids. There are 9 essential amino acids in total and some foods contain all of them – we call these complete proteins. Each amino acid has its own role in the body, ranging from supporting muscle growth and providing antibodies and important digestive enzymes to hormone production and much more.

Most children exceed their recommended daily intake of proteins, but here is an idea of some foods you can offer:

Complete proteins	Plant-based complete proteins	Incomplete proteins (not containing all 9 amino acids, but still good!)
Meat Fish Eggs Dairy	Quinoa Soy products, such as tofu Edamame beans Hemp seeds Flaxseed	Lentils Beans Nuts Seeds Peas Sweetcorn Asparagus Broccoli

1 portion = a serving the size of your baby's palm
Aim to offer 2 portions a day (or 3 if your baby follows a vegetarian diet)

The Importance of iron

When it comes to weaning, iron is the nutrient that sits above the rest. Think main character energy. Star player. The Beyoncé of micronutrients. Not only is it one of the main reasons we begin weaning at 6 months, it's also the most common nutrient for babies, children and adults alike to be deficient in. In a nutshell, we all benefit from an iron-rich diet, so any tips you pick up here can be applied to the whole family and continued... forever. Handy.

Babies in the womb get a delicious boost of iron in the third trimester to support the rapid growth and organ development that's taking place. They enter the world with a healthy reserve of this iron to keep them ticking over, but by the time they get to the 6-month mark, these stores begin to dwindle. Because of this, it's important to prioritise iron in your baby's meals and make sure they're offered iron-rich foods throughout the day.

The science

Iron is a mineral found in every single cell of the human body. It creates haemoglobin and myoglobin, two words that may or may not have just transported you back to your GCSE biology classroom. They're responsible for moving, storing and releasing oxygen around the body, so they're kind of a big deal. Because iron is vital to growth and development, it's really no surprise that it's so important when it comes to feeding our small humans that are growing and developing every millisecond of the day.

Why is iron important for adults?	Why is iron important for babies?
A lack of iron stores can lead to a drop in red blood cells, and a drop in red blood cells can lead to iron-deficiency anaemia. Symptoms of anaemia Fatigue, weakness Light-headedness Confusion, loss of concentration Sensitivity to cold Shortness of breath Rapid heartbeat Pale skin Hair loss, brittle nails	☑ Key in growth and development ☑ Essential for blood production ☑ Key in transporting oxygen around the body ☑ Helps to preserve the immune system ☑ Helps the regulation of body temperature ☑ Key in energy and focus In fact, studies have been carried out that link iron deficiency in school children with poorer memory, attention problems, social problems and higher scores in anxiety and depression compared to their peers.

Iron can be found in lots of different food sources and it comes in two forms: haem iron and non-haem iron. Haem iron comes from animal sources and is more readily absorbed by the body. Non-haem iron comes from plant sources and is less readily absorbed. If you have chosen a vegetarian diet for your baby you will need to include lots of plant-based iron-rich foods to maximise their intake of non-haem iron.

Here are some examples of iron-rich foods:

- Beef
- Dark meats on poultry
- Eggs
- Salmon
- Sweet potato
- Beans and pulses
- Lentils
- Edamame beans
- Peas
- Fortified oats
- Chia, hemp and flax seeds
- Tahini/sesame
- Dark leafy greens
- Broccoli

Vitamin C

If iron is the main character, then vitamin C is the loyal and devoted sidekick. Just like Batman and Robin, they should always be seen together. This is because vitamin C aids iron absorption, therefore maximising each meal's benefit to the body. Name a better duo!

Sources of vitamin C include:

- Citrus fruits, such as lemons and oranges
- Peppers
- Kiwi fruit
- Broccoli
- Cantaloupe melon
- Tomatoes
- Strawberries
- Potatoes
- Sweet potatoes
- Leafy greens

I could be here all day listing vitamins and nutrients, and explaining what they do for both you and your growing baby. Luckily, when we prioritise the wholesome foods listed in all the sections above, they contain an abundance of other good stuff for our bodies to make use of, such as:

- **Calcium:** used to build and maintain strong bones and teeth
- **Potassium:** promotes heart health and stimulates brain function
- **Magnesium:** helps to maintain healthy blood sugar levels and aids emotional regulation
- **B vitamins:** support red blood cell production and healthy brain development and function
- **Vitamin A:** promotes healthy vision and immune system
- **Vitamin D:** for healthy muscles, bones and teeth

Seeds!

I became obsessed with seeds during weaning, and with three types in particular: chia seeds, hemp seeds and flaxseed. These seeds are nutritional powerhouses and we now use them regularly in our meals as a family. They might not be common things you have in your kitchen, but let me explain why they are the perfect addition for your baby's weaning (and your diet, too!).

These three particular seeds are amazing because they pack a lot of nutritional benefits whilst being teeny tiny and not taking up too much space in your baby's tummy. Although seeds are fibrous, you don't need a lot of them to benefit. A sprinkle of hemp seeds on avocado, half a teaspoon of soaked chia seeds mixed into yoghurt or a tablespoon of flaxseed added to a baking recipe can really boost the goodness of a meal! They are good for hormone health, contain lots of key nutrients for weaning, such as iron, add complete protein to meals and are all a rich source of the omega 3 fats needed for healthy brain development.

Chia seeds

Look for 'chia seeds' (nice and easy). Chia seeds are full of antioxidants and they're also high in calcium, which is great for growing bones and teeth. They taste of nothing and have a gel-like texture once soaked.

17g protein per 100g

7.7mg iron per 100g

How to use them

Chia seeds must be soaked before eating, as they quickly swell on contact with liquid, and if they're eaten dry they will swell inside the body and cause digestive problems. Soak them in water, milk, plant-based milk or yoghurt for at least 30 minutes until the seeds turn gel-like. Make sure there is a ratio of at least 1 part chia seeds to 4 parts liquid (1 teaspoon of chia seeds should be soaked in at least 4 teaspoons of milk).

You also do not want to give your baby too much, as chia seeds are full of fibre! Start with a small amount and this can be gradually increased, but don't give more than 1 teaspoon per day.

You can also use chia seeds as an egg replacement in baking by making a chia egg. However, this will purely be to bind your recipe together as an egg would, because almost all nutrients of a chia seed are destroyed by cooking. For that reason, using a flax egg in baking is superior as you will get more nutritional benefit (see opposite for instructions about a flax egg). If you do want to make a chia egg, mix 1 tablespoon of chia seeds with 3 tablespoons of water and leave for 5–10 minutes to thicken.

Flaxseed

Look for 'ground brown' or 'ground golden' flaxseed. There is not much nutritional difference between the two, but I like using ground golden flaxseed because it doesn't alter the colour of my baking, whereas brown flaxseed will make muffins and cakes come out darker. Flaxseed doesn't have a distinct flavour, but it is mildly grainy in texture. For that reason I personally don't like it mixed into very smooth foods such as yoghurt, but in textured foods it's not noticeable.

18g protein per 100g

5.7mg iron per 100g

How to use it

Flaxseed is great mixed into porridge, in baking recipes and used to add grip to slippery foods. Unlike hemp and chia seeds, flaxseed stays stable in high heat, which means that it does not lose as many nutrients during cooking.

You can also use flaxseed as an egg replacement in baking by making a flax egg. Simply add 1 tablespoon of flaxseed to a cup with 3 tablespoons of boiling water, mix well and refrigerate for 10–15 minutes until it thickens to a gel. That amount replaces 1 egg, so scale up if the recipe calls for more than 1 egg.

Hemp seeds

Look for 'shelled' or 'hulled' hemp 'seeds' or 'hearts' – many names, all the same product. These seeds are small, soft discs with a very mild, nutty taste. Once mixed or sprinkled onto food, you can't really taste them at all!

30g protein per 100g

8mg iron per 100g

How to use them

Hemp seeds are great sprinkled onto toast toppings, mixed into porridge after cooking and as a way to add grip to slippery foods such as avocado. Hemp seeds go crispy when cooked and most of their omega oils are destroyed, so it's best to add them to foods post-cooking.

Note: Always aim to serve seeds alongside foods with some moisture. This allows the seeds to stick to the foods for easy eating. Where food is too dry, there is a risk of the seeds getting stuck in the throat. Offering sips of water throughout a meal also helps to wash down any seeds that may still be in the mouth.

Gagging vs choking

For parents approaching or in the midst of weaning, concerns over choking rank pretty highly in their list of worries. It's important to remember that instances of choking are thankfully very rare. Far more common (and the cause for a lot of confusion) is the gag reflex. Many parents mistake gagging for choking, so it's important to get to grips with the differences between them, as the approaches to the two are very different.

What's the difference?

GAGGING	CHOKING
• A natural reflex and a normal part of weaning • Tongue forward • Spluttering, coughing and/or heaving • Potential redness (although this won't apply to all skin tones) • Food will move forward in the mouth and the baby will continue their meal Airway clear	• There is a blockage and first aid is required • Tongue often in the mouth/pulled back • Quiet or silent; there may be some gasping/wheezing • Blueness (although this won't be immediately apparent on all skin tones) • The food will not move forward in the mouth and baby will likely look panicked Airway blocked – perform first aid

The gag reflex

Whilst the sight of our baby gagging can wreak havoc with our anxiety, I invite you to see the gag reflex as a friend and not a foe. It should be viewed as a positive thing: it is the mouth's defence mechanism against choking. When your baby is gagging, that is their body's way of saying 'Woah! More chewing needed' or 'No, you should not swallow that entire chicken chunk whole'.

The tough part is that at the start of weaning this same reflex will also be triggered by new tastes, textures and areas of the mouth being experienced that the body just isn't used to yet. When your baby starts weaning, the threshold for the gag reflex sits much further forwards on their tongue and it will be triggered easily. It's only with eating practice that this will begin to adjust. Even babies who are weaned on purées cannot escape this process, as it's reported that they struggle with gagging later down the line when moving on to finger foods. In the words of the children's literary classic *We're Going on a Bear Hunt*, 'You can't go over it. You can't go under it. You've got to go through it!'

When your baby gags, it is likely they will be unfazed. Follow their lead; stay calm and let them work it out. You can talk to them about what they're experiencing, 'That's broccoli, is that a new taste for you?' or if you suspect they have too much in their mouth, tell them so. You can lean forward and stick your tongue out to model getting food to drop out of your mouth. Over time they will build links between phrases like 'that's too much' and what it is they are experiencing.

What NOT to do

With gagging, resist the urge to get involved. Sit on your hands if you must! Take some deep breaths. Count to ten. Babies are attuned to your energy, and if your reaction to gagging is always frenzied panic, then they may begin to feel it's something to be scared of.

Above all, do not put your fingers into your baby's mouth to try to remove the food. There are a few key reasons for this:

1. Putting fingers into a baby's mouth has the potential to frighten or injure them.

2. An adult finger could push food into the baby's airway, therefore causing a blockage and escalating the gagging to choking.

3. The tissue in a baby's mouth and throat is very soft, and fingernails can easily scratch it. Fingernails also contain a lot of bacteria, which can transfer to any cuts and cause the soft tissue to swell. Swelling around a baby's airway can then result in breathing difficulties and a situation where emergency medical attention is required.

The best thing to do is to allow your baby to work it out for themselves. More often than not, the food will end up coming back out of their mouth after a few uncomfortable seconds (even if it feels like much longer!). If you are worried because your baby is really struggling with a large piece of food (gagging it forwards and then repeating the process over and over again), you can calmly fish the food from the front of their mouth when they bring it forwards. Never put your fingers into their mouth any further than your nail bed.

> **Note from a nutritionist: Gagging and vomiting** – A baby gagging with vomit is worrying, but it can sometimes happen when baby starts solids. This is because some babies have a very sensitive gag reflex that causes them to bring food up when they gag. This is more common in babies with a history of reflux. If baby continues to gag and vomit after most meals, or becomes upset after gagging and starts to reject solid meals as a result, consult your GP for further advice and guidance.

Choking

Choking refers to 'when someone's airway suddenly gets blocked, either fully or partly, so they can't breathe or breathe properly' (NHS website).

In young children especially, choking can occur not only with food but as a result of swallowing small household objects or toy parts, and the choking risk remains the same whether a baby is spoon-fed or adopting baby-led weaning. Please don't think I'm saying this to worry you – choking incidents still remain very rare. There is so much you can do to reduce the risk: serving foods safely, giving meals in a safe eating environment (in a stable highchair, not moving around) and, of course, always staying with your baby throughout a meal.

As well as following all the right steps for safety, I am a huge champion of taking a baby and child first aid course. These cover a range of topics and it reduced my anxiety massively to feel that bit more prepared for what steps I should take if something were to go wrong (not just in weaning, but in caring for a child in general). I have a great partnership with St John Ambulance, who have put together a hub of free resources and videos on family first aid. I highly recommend taking the time to go through them to either learn the skills or refresh your knowledge if you've previously done a course, and to share them widely with grandparents or anybody else who may be looking after your child. You can find all of the resources at *sja.org.uk/moonandrue*.

Common choking hazards

An infant's windpipe is small in diameter and soft compared to an adult's. For these reasons, there are certain foods that pose more of a risk and should be modified (or avoided) while children are small.

Other non-food-related choking hazards to be aware of are coins, batteries, magnets, latex balloons, marbles, toy parts, beads, rings, buttons and small stones.

HAZARD	WHY?	WHAT TO DO
Blueberries	Firm, round objects can easily become lodged in the windpipe	Squish blueberries to flatten them. Whole unflattened blueberries can be introduced from 12 months, with careful supervision and encouragement of chewing.
Grapes, cherries	Firm and round	Cut these fruits into quarters or sixths (into segment shapes by cutting in half lengthways, and then repeating on each half). For 6-month-olds, peel off any thick skin. Due to them being very firm, it's best to cut these fruits until at least the age of 5.

HAZARD	WHY?	WHAT TO DO
Hard, raw fruit and veg such as carrot and apple	Hard, crunchy texture which is difficult to chew	In early weaning, cook fruit and veg until it is soft enough to easily smush between your forefinger and thumb. You can progress to serving these foods raw, grated from 9 months and then thinly sliced from around 12 months. Check the Solid Starts food database (solidstarts.com/foods) for specific safe serving suggestions for each food.
Sausages, hot dogs, etc	Springy texture, rounded	Processed meats aren't the best for a little one's diet due to their salt content, so you could avoid these altogether. But if you are serving low-salt sausages, cut them into quarters rather than rounds and remove the skin of the sausage for babies younger than 18 months.
Nuts and large seeds	Hard to chew	Nuts and large seeds should always be finely chopped or ground before serving, or offered as a nut butter instead. Whole nuts should not be offered to a child until they're 5 years old.
Peanut butter	Thick texture that can clog together in the throat	Keep layers of peanut butter thin and do not serve in dollops that could be scooped and eaten in one go. Peanut butter can also be thinned out with some milk, formula or breast milk if desired.
Dry chia seeds	Can bond and clump together on contact with moisture	Always soak chia seeds for at least 30 minutes before serving in a ratio of 1:4 (4 times as much liquid as seeds) and ensure you stir the soaked seeds thoroughly before serving. A small sprinkle of chia seeds on yoghurt should also be left for at least 30 minutes before serving.
Popcorn	A mixture of textures, including hard kernels, which are difficult to chew	There is very little you can do to adapt popcorn in order to make it safer to eat, so it is advised to avoid it until the age of 5.
Marshmallows	Gelatinous texture which can glue together in the airway	Marshmallows may seem like a child-friendly option, but they are actually high-risk as they are incredibly difficult to dislodge from the airway even when following first aid. They are also very high in sugar, so they are best avoided until at least the age of 5.
Hard-boiled sweets, lollipops, etc	Round, firm and easily accidentally swallowed	As these foods are both a high choking risk and high in sugar, they are best avoided until at least the age of 5.

Safe serving

When serving foods for baby-led weaning, you want to make sure they are both easy for your little one to access and safe in terms of reducing choking risk. There are some great resources online, such as the Solid Starts food database (see previous page) and NHS website, which give guidance on ways to serve individual foods to each age group. If you're unsure, search '[Food]-safe ways to serve at [baby's age in months]' and a wealth of guidance will be at your fingertips!

Here are some general rules of thumb to factor in when serving foods:

6–9 months	Developmentally, your baby will use a **palmar grasp** (holding food in their fists). Pieces of food should be at least the size of an adult finger to ensure your baby can achieve successful self-feeding. They will hold the finger slices and tear off bites with their gums. Avoid serving food in small chunks at this stage, as with a palmar grasp these chunks will be scooped and stuffed into their mouths (increasing choking risk). Food should be cooked until it can be easily smushed between forefinger and thumb.* Your baby is not experienced with chewing and may not yet have any teeth, so a soft and squishable texture is appropriate. *Meats will not be smushable but should be given in large slices (the size of an adult finger).
9–12 months	Your baby should be developing their **pincer grip** by now (the ability to pick up food between their finger and thumb). You can now offer smaller, bite-sized chunks of food. They don't need every food item cut into tiny pieces, it's advisable to still offer some foods in finger slices to give them a range of eating practice. Most food should still be cooked until soft and smushable. Some foods, such as apple and carrot, can be served grated, and by 12 months in thin slices.
What's it like?	If you're not sure how to safely serve a food, consider what other food it is similar to in texture and firmness. For example, large or firm raspberries should be approached similarly to blueberries and flattened before serving. Firm pears or plums should be steamed as you would apples. And as with grapes, cherry tomatoes should be cut into quarters or sixths, with any thick skin removed.

Portion sizes and appetites

In the early days of our TikTok journey, I could pretty much guarantee that on every video there would be an equal sprinkling of comments saying either:

'That's far too much! Your baby is going to be overweight.'

Or,

'Is that all you're giving her? Your baby must be starving!'

On the face of it these comments were irritating at best and ignorant at worst, especially because, as the parent, you are often already wary of whether you've got the portion size right and how much is eaten. But comments like these are reflective of a wider anxiety – people just aren't sure how much food a baby should be having.

The problem is, as with everything else in parenting, there is no magic formula that you can take and apply to every baby. Each baby is different and it's pointless to attempt to compare how much one baby eats to another, so try not to allow these thoughts to enter your head. Portion size is only one side of the deal, the other equally important factor is your baby's appetite. Unless you have a particularly advanced 6-month-old, it's unlikely that they are going to be able to explain to you how much they fancy eating that day. Their appetites will change from meal to meal, and whenever they enter different phases: they will have growth spurts, they will have periods of being a bottomless pit and they will have periods where trying to encourage a meal past

their lips is harder than trying to enter Fort Knox. As parents, it is our job to offer the food, it is up to your baby how much they choose to eat.

Try to be as flexible as you can and don't put too much pressure on yourself or your baby. As weaning progresses, you will get used to how much food they might roughly eat in one sitting. But there will still be days where they eat much less, or days when you think they might like seconds. Babies are intuitive eaters, they do not naturally eat to excess.

I have included rough portion serving sizes for carbs, fats and protein on pages 22–25. These are based on the size of your baby's hand, which is helpful as hands grow with us! As for the amount of meals you should offer each day, I followed the timeline below and found it worked well. It gave Rue time to adjust to her solids intake and it gave me time to adjust to planning for and making more meals as time went on.

NHS guidance:

6 months	1 meal a day to start, working up to more
7–9 months	2 or 3 meals a day
10–12 months	3 meals a day consistently
12 months+	3 meals a day plus 2 snacks

What this looked like for us

(Remember, all babies will be different, but this should give you some insight into how we tried to follow Rue's lead and stay flexible.)

6 months – For around the first three weeks of weaning we offered one meal a day. I experimented with different mealtimes, switching between breakfasts, lunches and dinners throughout this period. In her early meals, Rue would only take a few bites, but this gradually increased day by day.

7 months – By this time we had begun to offer two meals a day. Because I had experimented with different mealtimes, I'd learnt that Rue found morning meals more challenging (not a breakfast girlie at this point), so I would usually offer lunch and dinner. As time went on I increased the size of these meals.

8.5 months – We began to add in a third meal. Rue was still very much a moody Margaret in the mornings; she was less engaged with the meal and would lose interest quickly. So I kept breakfast meals small and manageable. She also started to eat less of her lunch and dinner meals because she was having more overall in the day. It was also around this time that we began to reduce her milk feeds (more on that on page 39).

10–11 months – By this time we were offering three appropriate-sized meals a day. By 'appropriate', I mean in line with her appetite and in response to her hunger and fullness cues. She had also done a U-turn on her previous opinion of breakfast – it was now her favourite meal of the day!

Rue started teething at 10 months, and in the days around a tooth cutting her appetite was massively affected (this is common), so I kept meals small and manageable during this time and served soft and/or cooling foods.

12 months – We started to introduce snacks. Rue was not particularly bothered by snacking and still did the majority of her eating at mealtimes. Snacks became more of a regular fixture by the time she reached 14 months.

Key tips

You can find more detail on the points below in the Troubleshooting section on page 48, but here are a few great bits of advice that helped me to better understand portions and appetites:

▶ Remember that in the first few months of weaning your baby is still relying on their milk feeds for fullness and nutrients. Any added iron and healthy fats they get from solids is a bonus.

▶ Look out for fullness cues, such as playing with food or looking disinterested, to know when your baby is finished with a meal.

▶ Don't focus too heavily on their intake at each individual meal instead, take an overview of the week's meals.

▶ Reframe thinking of meals as 'an expectation to eat' to 'an opportunity to eat'.

Milk

The relationship between milk feeds and weaning meals is one that can cause a lot of confusion, but don't worry too much as all changes are gradual and you don't need to change anything at the beginning of weaning. At 6 months, continue to give your baby the same milk feeds they had been having up to this point. If you are breastfeeding, continue to breastfeed on demand. If you are bottle feeding, you should give them the same number of bottles of infant formula as they had previously. This is why you will often see early weaning referred to as 'complementary feeding' – these first foods are given in addition to the milk that makes up most of their diet.

Over time, milk intake reduces as more of their nutrient needs are met from solid foods (and they are fuller from these meals). Picture some old-school weighing scales with 'milk' on one side and 'food' on the other. At the beginning of weaning, your baby is relying mostly on milk, so the milk side of the scales is weighed down a lot, but over time the weight gradually shifts to the other side, bit by bit. As your baby becomes more efficient and engaged with eating solid foods, the food side of the scales gets heavier and the milk side becomes lighter.

The timings of your meals will depend on a variety of things, including how many naps a day your baby is taking at any given time. I've included some schedules below, but try to find a rhythm that works for you and your baby.

The next page shows a rough template of what the balance between milk and food might look like.

> **Note from a nutritionist: Plant-based milks** – Dairy milk is nutritionally far superior to plant-based alternatives, so include this unless your baby shows an intolerance. When it comes to plant-based milks, soya milk is the most nutritious, but there are concerns about this because of the high levels of plant oestrogens in soy. If you're using oat milk or almond milk, ensure that it's unsweetened and fortified. Never use rice milk, because of the high levels of arsenic.

AGE	DAILY MILK	DAILY FOOD	WHEN/HOW
6 months	Breastfed on demand or 500–600ml of infant formula	1 meal	Leave at least 1 hour between solids and milk so your baby is hungry. Don't offer solids too close to a nap, to allow your little one time to digest it and yourself time to observe any reactions.
7–9 months	Breastfed on demand or 500–600ml of infant formula	2–3 meals	Leave at least 1 hour between solids and milk so your baby is hungry. For example, milk on waking, breakfast a couple of hours later.
10 months	Breastfed on demand or 400ml a day of infant formula	3 meals	Aim to always offer solids before milk feeds; for example, breakfast on waking, milk before nap. As before, leave time between solids and offering milk. If your baby consistently doesn't finish their milk, this is a sign you can reduce the amount offered, or drop a milk feed altogether (ensuring you do not drop multiple milk feeds at once).

12 months	Breastfed on demand or 360ml a day of infant formula or cow's milk or 3 portions of dairy per day	3 meals, 2 snacks	From 12 months you can introduce cow's milk as a drink. It is advisable to begin to offer milk feeds in a cup, rather than a bottle.
			
			Your baby can also have their dairy needs met through the food they eat. One portion of dairy can look like:
			  80g of plain yoghurt
			  15g of cheese
			
			Other good sources of calcium and iodine are:
			  Tinned sardines and salmon
			  Nut butters
			
			Other good sources of calcium are:
			  Oranges
			  Fortified breakfast cereals

2–3 years	3 portions of dairy per day		Toddlers at this age might drink 2 small cups of milk per day if it is a drink they enjoy. They should have a range of healthy dairy sources in their diet such as cheese, yoghurt and fromage frais. From 2 years old, little ones can be moved onto semi-skimmed milk if desired. Skimmed or 1% milk still isn't recommended as it doesn't contain enough fat.

Milk and solids feeding schedule

Here are some example schedules of how to time your milk feeds and solid feeds. These aren't templates, they are just offering some guidance to help you establish your routine – you will find your own rhythm based on your baby's sleep schedule, appetite and what works best for your household! I've shaded in the solid feeds so that you can clearly see how you will move from very little solids (and lots of milk!) at 6 months, to gradually relying on more solids over time.

6-MONTH-OLD EXAMPLE SCHEDULE, 1 MEAL A DAY AND 3 NAPS	
	Wake up - milk feed
	Nap
	Wake up - lunch
	Milk feed
	Nap
	Wake up - milk feed
	Short nap
	Wake up - milk feed
	Bedtime milk feed

7-MONTH-OLD EXAMPLE SCHEDULE, 2 MEALS A DAY AND 3 NAPS	
	Wake up - breakfast
	Milk feed
	Nap
	Wake up - lunch
	Milk feed
	Nap
	Wake up - milk feed
	Nap*
	Wake up - milk feed
	Bedtime milk feed

*Based on a 7-month-old still on 3 naps. Some will have reduced to 2 naps, in which case your day might look more like the schedule on the next page.

10-MONTH-OLD EXAMPLE SCHEDULE, 3 MEALS A DAY AND 2 NAPS	
	Wake up - milk feed
	Breakfast
	Nap
	Wake up - milk feed
	Lunch
	Nap
	Wake up - milk feed
	Dinner
	Bedtime milk feed

15-MONTH-OLD EXAMPLE SCHEDULE, 3 MEALS A DAY, 2 SNACKS AND 1 EARLY MIDDAY NAP	
	Wake up
	Breakfast
	Snack with milk (in a cup)
	Nap
	Lunch on waking
	Snack
	Dinner
	Bedtime milk feed (in a cup)

12-MONTH-OLD EXAMPLE SCHEDULE, 3 MEALS A DAY, 2 SNACKS AND 2 NAPS	
	Wake up
	Breakfast
	Snack and milk offered in a cup
	Nap
	Lunch
	Snack and milk offered in a cup
	Nap
	Dinner
	Bedtime milk feed (in a cup)

20-MONTH-OLD EXAMPLE SCHEDULE, 3 MEALS A DAY, 2 SNACKS AND 1 LATER MIDDAY NAP	
	Wake up
	Breakfast
	Snack
	Lunch
	Milk (in a cup)
	Nap
	Snack
	Dinner
	Bedtime milk feed (in a cup)

Allergens

On top of everything else there is to learn about weaning, the whole subject of allergens can feel like one piece of homework too much! The good news is, the likelihood of your little one having a food allergy remains relatively small, with around only 5–8% of babies and toddlers experiencing one. Another piece of good news is that within that percentage, many of those children will grow out of allergies, such as cow's milk and egg, by the time they reach 4 years old.

Introducing allergens

All that said, it's important to introduce allergens individually, to make sure you can identify any allergies early on. It's much better to stagger introducing them at the start of weaning than to rely on guesswork and eliminations further down the line. Follow my First Month of Weaning Plan at the back of this book (page 202) for a planned template of how to introduce eight of the most common allergens.

Some key things to know:

1. People can experience immediate (IgE) reactions, which occur within 30 minutes of consuming the food, or delayed (Non-IgE) reactions, which can occur any time up to 72 hours after eating.

2. Severe allergic reaction (anaphylaxis) does not occur on the first exposure to the food. The first exposure simply establishes the allergy, it will be exposures after this that cause a severe reaction to take place.

3. Some allergies, such as egg and peanut allergies, are related. Children with an egg allergy are at a higher risk of being allergic to peanuts. Children with eczema are at a higher risk of both egg and peanut allergies.

4. If you or your baby's other biological parent have a specific food allergy, you should seek medical advice before introducing that food. For infants at a high risk of developing an allergy, the advice is that early introduction is key, even as early as 4 months old (with the specific guidance of a healthcare professional).

Think of the allergen food as a rowdy person in a bar, and the body's immune system the bouncers. The first time the rowdy person comes in, they cause some irritation but nothing much happens. But the second (or maybe even third, fourth, fifth, etc.) time the rowdy person shows up, the bouncers recognise them and say 'We're not happy about you being here' and pile in aggressively, in an effort to remove them. This aggressive response from the body is the severe allergic reaction. The body launches antibodies to fight against the unwanted allergen.

The main allergens in the UK are:

- Cow's milk
- Egg (only Red Lion-stamped eggs should be eaten lightly cooked)
- Cereals containing gluten, such as wheat, barley and rye
- Peanuts and tree nuts (should always be served ground or as a nut butter)
- Seeds such as sesame, mustard and poppy (should always be served ground or as a paste, such as tahini)
- Soya
- Fish
- Shellfish and molluscs (do not serve raw or lightly cooked)
- Celery and celeriac

When introducing an allergen, you should start with a very small amount, such as:

- 1 teaspoon of hard-boiled egg (including the white and the yolk) mashed with some breastmilk or formula
- 1 teaspoon of dairy yoghurt
- A pea-sized amount of peanut butter mixed with some mashed banana

Offer the allergen for a few consecutive days, ideally at meals earlier in the day to give you time to observe for reactions. Do not introduce multiple allergens at once so that if a reaction does occur, it is clearer as to which one has caused it. Reactions to look out for include:

Immediate reactions (IgE) Within 30 minutes of exposure	Delayed reactions (Non-IgE) Up to 72 hours after exposure
Breathing problems such as wheezing, asthma or difficulty breathing Skin problems such as redness and/or swelling caused by hives or rashes, or eczema worsening suddenly Diarrhoea Vomiting	Tummy or toilet problems such as tummy pain, wind, bloating and diarrhoea Delayed vomiting and/or reflux Eczema flare-ups Ongoing wheezing

Once an allergen has been introduced, if there's no reaction you can gradually increase the amount you offer. You should then aim to keep up exposures to that food regularly in your baby's diet. If there is a reaction, reach out to your doctor for guidance on the next steps. Some foods, such as milk and egg, have dietary 'ladders' that you can follow to re-introduce the allergen safely at a time in the future. Make sure you speak with your doctor, health visitor or a nutritionist or dietitian for specific support and guidance with this.

Keeping up with the allergens

The most up-to-date advice is that early introduction to allergenic foods, followed by regular exposures, can reduce the likelihood of an allergy developing. So, parents, the answer is SIMPLE – just include all the common allergens a couple of times a week in your baby's diet and you'll be fine... easy!

Except, no. No, it's not.

It's another example of parenting advice that might look great on paper but in reality is quite hard to execute. I don't know about you, but I am not in the habit of serving Rue a few meals a week with oysters, celeriac and mustard seeds.

So, what can we do? Well, out of the main allergens, there are a few key ones you should prioritise. Some are popular in most diets and can be incorporated without even thinking about it. Some are commonly hidden as an ingredient in many foods and so should be introduced even if you don't think they're a regular feature in your weekly shop. And some are actually best left alone until they're a little older...

Here are my top tips for allergens to prioritise, and some easy ways to include them in your baby's diet:

ALLERGEN	WHAT TO KNOW	HOW TO KEEP UP EXPOSURES
The Big 3: gluten, dairy and eggs	These need little introduction! They are common ingredients found in a range of everyday foods and meals.	• Gluten – bread, pasta, cereals containing wheat, rye, barley and oats* • Dairy – cheese, yoghurt, cow's milk (in recipes under 12 months and as a drink over 12 months) • Eggs – in baking recipes and pancakes, or hard-boiled, scrambled and in omelettes *Oats are naturally gluten-free but are commonly manufactured alongside products that contaminate them with gluten. Buy oats labelled 'gluten-free' if you are aiming to avoid this allergen.
Peanuts	Stick to peanut butter rather than whole nuts and, once introduced, aim to give your little one 2g of peanut butter, 3 times a week. Peanuts are not actually nuts, they're legumes, which is why they are separate from tree nuts in the world of allergies.	• On porridge, pancakes or toast • Spread over fruits and berries such as banana, flattened raspberries and strawberries • Peanut butter* mixed with yoghurt or cream cheese as a dip or spread *Ensure your serve peanut butter in thin layers, as thick layers and clumps pose a choking risk.

ALLERGEN	WHAT TO KNOW	HOW TO KEEP UP EXPOSURES
Soya	Soya is sneakily in 60% of manufactured goods! Breads, pastries, soups, cereals, energy bars, baby foods – even some tinned fish and meat products may contain traces.	• Plain firm tofu cut into fingers is often a hit with newly weaning babies • Firm tofu pan-fried in seasonings of your choice • Silken tofu can be mixed with fruit purée, or unsweetened cocoa and berries for a little chocolatey pud • Edamame beans – buy frozen and shelled to easily add to dishes. Whole beans are a choking hazard, squeeze them between your forefinger and thumb to split them into halves before serving
Tree nuts	Tree nut allergy refers to almonds, Brazil nuts, cashew nuts, hazelnuts, walnuts, pecans, pistachios and macadamia nuts.	Use nut butters and incorporate them into all the suggestions given above for peanut butter. The annoying thing about tree nuts is that they don't come as a group – someone could be allergic to one type, some of them or all of them. It's not realistic to have 200 different nut butters in your cupboard at any given time, but just be intentional about trying some out, prioritising the nuts you would typically eat in your household.
Sesame seeds	Sesame allergies are becoming more and more common in the UK and, similar to soy, sesame and sesame oil are used in products you wouldn't expect.	• Houmous and pitta bread (check out my Homemade Houmous recipe on page 66) • Houmous and veggie sticks • Tahini* as a replacement wherever you would use a nut butter • Tahini mixed into desserts or drizzled on fruits *Tahini is a great cupboard staple. Even once opened, it can be stored in the cupboard and will be fine for at least a few months. Give it a stir before use to combine the sesame paste and the oils, and you're good to go!
Fish	Protein, omega 3s, vitamin D, B12, haem iron, zinc, magnesium, the list goes on. Fish is that girl, she's got it all, so you should definitely aim to include it in your baby's diet. According to the NHS, you can give boys up to 4 portions of oily fish a week, but it is best to give girls no more than 2 portions a week.	• White fish like cod, haddock and pollock cooked and offered in finger slices (dunk in egg and breadcrumbs before cooking for homemade fish fingers) • My Fish and Veggie Curry (page 160) • My Salmon Veggie Pancakes (page 102) • Tinned sardines are a great oily fish option and are more affordable than salmon

ALLERGEN	WHAT TO KNOW	HOW TO KEEP UP EXPOSURES
Celery	On its own, raw celery is a choking hazard due to its shape and firmness.	• Finely slice it and add it to soups and pasta sauces like my Iron-rich Lentil Pasta Sauce! (page 64)
Celeriac	Those who suffer from celery allergy are likely to also be allergic to celeriac.	• Can be cooked and mashed as a side with meals
Shellfish and molluscs	Shellfish, such as prawns and crab; molluscs, such as mussels and oysters. If serving to children they must be properly cooked, not lightly cooked or raw.	Prawns can be a choking hazard and both prawn and crab are naturally high in sodium, so it's best to wait until after your baby's first birthday to introduce them. If you're serving molluscs to your baby you are doing more than me, that's for sure! Similar to crustaceans, it's best to wait until your little one is older. Mussels and oysters carry higher risk of foodborne illness and also contain cadmium, which is a toxic metal that can impact brain development. For these reasons, please take care if offering them to your baby and do so in moderation.

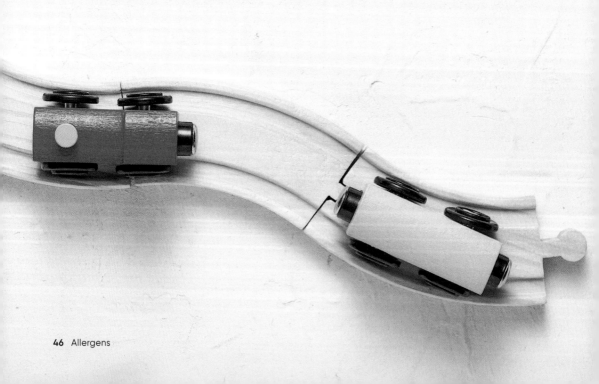

TLDR: The crash course summary

- Baby-led weaning builds chewing and swallowing skills, encourages intuitive eating and develops motor skills.

- Never give your baby added salt or sugar, honey, low-fat dairy products or too many wholegrains.

- A stable footrest is a key feature of an effective highchair.

- Introduce open cups and straw cups to offer water alongside weaning meals.

- Your baby needs to show three signs of readiness before you can begin weaning: bringing food to their mouth, sitting unassisted, and the loss of their tongue-thrust reflex.

- Make sure you include a range of iron-rich foods in your baby's diet, alongside foods containing vitamin C.

- The gag reflex is a positive thing and is not the same as choking. Never put your fingers into your baby's mouth to remove food.

- The common choking hazards on page 30 should always be adapted or avoided.

- Search '[Food]-safe ways to serve at [baby's age in months]' if you're ever unsure about how to offer a food.

- The size of your baby's meals should be determined using a balance of guideline portion sizes and baby's appetite.

- Sudden losses of appetite can often be down to teething or illness, and these phases will pass.

- Snacks can be introduced from 12 months.

- Think of meals as an opportunity to eat, rather than an expectation to eat.

- Keep milk feeds the same until your baby becomes more efficient with eating.

- Look out for both immediate and delayed allergic reactions.

- Severe allergic reactions (anaphylaxis) are unlikely to happen the first time a food is eaten, it will be an exposure after this where a severe reaction might occur.

- The main allergens are: cow's milk, egg, gluten, peanuts, tree nuts, seeds (especially sesame), soya, fish, shellfish and molluscs, celery and celeriac.

Troubleshooting:
Common weaning worries

How do I know when my baby has had enough?

⭐ Look out for fullness cues to know when your baby is finished with a meal. These can include:

- playing with food
- dropping food from their highchair
- daydreaming or looking disinterested in the meal
- spitting food out/closing the mouth when food is offered

I feel like they've eaten hardly anything!

⭐ For phases when your baby is eating less, or meal refusal, avoid focusing too heavily on their intake at each individual meal. Instead, take an overview of a few days, or better still, the week's, meals, and it is likely you will see that when you add it all together, they have been eating. Even if it hasn't been as much as you would like.

⭐ Reframe thinking of meals as 'an expectation to eat' to 'an opportunity to eat'. As the old saying goes, you can lead a horse to water but you can't make him drink. You can lead your baby to a wonderful plate-of-food-that-you've-spent-time-in-the-kitchen-lovingly-preparing, but you can't force them to eat it!

My baby doesn't seem interested in eating at all.

⭐ Eat with your baby so that they get plenty of modelling of what to do. Keep meals small and manageable, eat the same food as them and make it look great! Show them what to do but don't put any pressure on them.

⭐ Try to offer meals before a milk feed, rather than after, to allow hunger to be a driving force in getting them to engage with a meal.

My baby is a really slow eater. Every meal is taking us ages!

⭐ On some occasions, slow eating could be a sign that your baby is full (if they begin at a regular pace but gradually become slower), however, most of the time it is simply because your baby is learning new skills and that can take time. Try to give yourself plenty of time for each meal, especially in the first 6 weeks or so of weaning. As they become more efficient with eating they will speed up, but they need a bit of grace and patience in the early days while they're working everything out. While they're still having plenty of milk, you can afford to keep portion sizes smaller if you need a shorter mealtime, just make sure you're still prioritising iron-rich foods.

She used to eat everything, now she just finishes her fruit and refuses the rest.

⭐ Remember, your baby is eating from what is available on the plate. If you are often finding yourself in situations where your baby eats all of their fruit and then refuses the rest of their meal, consider offering half, or even a third of their overall fruit serving at first. Allow hunger to be a driver to encourage them onto the other parts of the meal. You can always give the remainder of the fruit portion when you feel they've made good headway on some other food groups, but try not to do this in a way that frames the fruit as a reward for eating. You might simply add some more onto their plate without saying much, or offer them some more of a few different food items on the plate, 'You're nearly finished! Would you like a bit more chicken and a bit more kiwi fruit?'. If they choose not to eat the seconds of chicken, that is okay!

My toddler only wants snacks, never meals.

★ There are many different factors at play here, ranging from the formality of a meal in a highchair, to the pressure/overwhelm they might feel at a full plate, to the options of foods served. One thing I would say is to try to avoid offering too many 'beige' snacks, as toddlers will naturally gravitate towards them. As adults, we know a snack is a snack and a meal is a meal, but to a toddler it is simply 'Food I Have Been Offered'. If we always offer sweet, beige snacks but then expect them to eat vegetables, sauces and new flavours at mealtimes, you can see how this can lead to conflict. Aim to include a variety of colours and textures during snack time as well to avoid this – I've put some ideas together on page 164.

★ During meals, ensure there are some 'safe' foods on the plate. These are foods you know your toddler will enjoy – it can really help to get the ball rolling. Try to eat together as much as you can; even if your toddler does not engage with the meal, speak with them while you eat and allow them to be part of the experience. Don't put too much pressure on making them eat, toddlers will rebel against this energy!

★ I've put some ideas of ways to engage toddlers in mealtimes on page 145 (Stage 4 'fussy' eating).

They've been eating really well, but have suddenly lost their appetite over the last couple of days.

★ Usually the culprit for this is either illness or teething is imminent. Continue to offer a range of foods and you can even offer smaller meals with more regularity if you think that would be more manageable for your little one. During teething, or illnesses such as hand, foot and mouth, soft foods like scrambled eggs, and cold foods such as my Tropical Yoghurt Bark on page 112 can be very soothing to a sore mouth. Both of these instances should be a short-lived phase and they will be back to their usual selves once the illness has passed.

They love throwing their food on the floor.

★ Babies aged between 4 and 7 months old are learning about object permanence. This is the understanding that when an object is out of eyesight, it still exists. This skill is being consolidated by the time they reach 8 months, so it's quite common for babies to experiment with throwing food from their highchair (and peering at the masterpiece they are making on your floor) as part of perfecting this understanding. For babies beyond this age, it can simply be a case of enjoying the cause and effect – particularly if they get a good reaction from you! Some parents like to use a 'no thank you' plate on the highchair tray, where you use an empty plate (or leave a section on a weaning plate empty) and encourage your little one to put the unwanted food item there, rather than ejecting it from the highchair altogether. Mainly, try not to overly react to this behaviour, as that can encourage it further. It will pass and you can rest assured they won't reach adulthood and still consider it normal behaviour!

My baby won't put food in his mouth. It seems to go everywhere but!

⭐ If you are in early weaning, consider whether your baby is showing the signs of readiness to begin. If you're confident that they are, continue to offer small meals (just a few food items) and ensure you are eating with them to model what they should do. Remember that touching, smelling and seeing the food is all part of the learning experience too, so it's never a waste of time in terms of their development.

He keeps stuffing too much food into his mouth!

⭐ Food stuffing is a common developmental phase and very normal. Babies are building an internal mental image of their mouth, and filling it with as much food as possible gives great sensory feedback for this. They're trying to understand how much space they have in there, and what the different parts of their mouth feel like. Rest assured it's a phase that will pass eventually, although it does tend to swing in and out of their eating behaviours well into toddlerhood.

⭐ You should never put your fingers into their mouth to remove the food, but what you can do is consistently use phrases such as 'that's too much!' or lean forward and stick your tongue out to model how they can drop food out of their mouth. It's most likely that your little one will either gag on the food as it is too much to swallow, or they will realise themselves (after a few moments of discomfort) that they can't do much with a mouth that full and will spit some out.

My baby gags a lot unless it's a very smooth texture.

⭐ Some babies will gag a lot in the earlier stages of weaning (and some continue to for a good while!). As long as your baby is not upset, continue as normal with offering chunkier textures and finger foods. If you gravitate to serving only smooth textures, you will simply be prolonging this adjustment period.

They won't try anything new.

⭐ For younger babies, give them plenty of exposures and opportunities to experience food and don't write anything off. Show them how to eat it, show them that you are enjoying it, be patient and trust the process. It can take up to 20 times of trying a food for a baby to decide whether they like it, so providing plenty of opportunities is key.

⭐ Around the age of 12 months, food neophobia (fear of new foods) can set in, which means toddlers become more wary of new foods, or even foods they haven't had in a little while. It's a normal developmental phase and, although frustrating, is best managed by continuing to offer foods and not shying away from giving your toddler something even if you think they might reject it. Try to balance their plate so that there are some 'safe' foods and some 'new' foods and eat with them to show them it's enjoyable. They might like to eat some from your plate to get the ball rolling (food stolen from someone else is always better, right?). Most of all, try not to narrow down what you offer them as this can be a really tricky problem to try to fix later down the line.

Why does my baby keep spitting out food?

⭐ Make sure your baby has lost their tongue-thrust reflex and is properly ready to begin weaning. It might be that you need to wait a week or two more, and then come back to solids and try again.

It looks like my baby hates what I'm feeding them.

★ When it comes to your baby's reactions to food, you pretty much need to throw away all knowledge you would apply to interpreting an adult's behaviour. They will potentially gag, shudder and/or have a face of absolute disgust during some of their meals – all of this is normal. It's not a comment on your cooking and not a sign that they don't like what they are eating. Eating solids is a brand new experience and they are overloaded with new sensations. And, as we know, they are also liberated from any sense of 'manners' or 'politeness', so they're not going to adapt their facial features to spare your feelings! It can take 20 tastes of a food for them to decide whether they like it or not, and even these likes and dislikes will change as they progress through childhood, so keep offering a wide diet and have an open mind. Even if your baby cries during a meal, it is more likely to be out of surprise at a new sensation, or a lack of resilience due to tiredness, than being down to a dislike of a particular food.

My baby has been constipated.

★ This is common when starting solids. Without painting too much of a mental picture for you, you should prepare yourself for some seriously weird nappies! Constipation one minute, soft poos the next, it's all part of the fun of their bodies getting used to digesting solid foods. Just remember that diarrhoea straight after a meal, or consistently after eating a particular food, can be a sign of food allergy and should be discussed with your doctor.

★ Although prunes are a common remedy for adults, they are too harsh for a baby's digestive tract to be used in this way. Instead, offer very ripe (brown-spotted) bananas to relieve constipation but avoid serving bananas that are too yellow (just ripe) as these can make constipation worse.

How much water should my baby be having? Is tap water okay?

★ In the UK, tap water is considered safe from 6 months onwards (if you're elsewhere, you should check your local advice). Your baby will still be getting hydration from their milk feeds, so they do not need loads of drinking water. You can offer sips of water alongside their solid meals from an open cup or straw cup.

I was told solids would help them sleep better, but my baby's sleep has been disrupted since we started weaning.

★ Just as with their nappies, it's possible you will see changes in your baby's sleep as they adjust to eating solids. This can be down to the developmental leaps they are taking, as well as them adjusting to the sensations of digesting foods. It certainly isn't true that giving your baby solids will guarantee better sleep, which is why their sleep habits are not considered to have anything to do with the signs of readiness for weaning.

Pre-weaning checklist

Excited? Overwhelmed? Anxious? Feeling all the feels?! All totally normal. Weaning is a big deal! Here's a list of activities and ideas to get you and your baby ready and raring to go.

Set up your highchair – start to get used to this new piece of furniture. Work out the best position for it and give your baby some practice sitting in it.

Defrost your freezer – this is me passing on a deep regret because I so wish I'd done this before weaning! Eat up, clear out and defrost so that your freezer is organised and ready to store endless batch-cooked meals and snacks!

Buy the basics – I've included a list of items on page 16 that I think are great for starting weaning. My advice would be, don't go mad. Keep it minimal until you get a feel for what your baby really needs.

Practise a few recipes – you could eat them yourself or freeze them for when the time comes. Things like pancakes can be frozen for up to three months and are great for the early weaning days. If you're excited to get going, it's the perfect way to get ahead of the game!

Let your little one join you for mealtimes – I'm sure your baby has watched you eat many a sausage roll on the couch by now (no? Just me then...). From around 5 months, it's a great idea to get their highchair area set up and allow them to join you at the table while you eat a small meal. Give them teething toys, or one of their spoons and bowls, and talk to them while you eat. This will set the tone for the routine of mealtimes, then by the time you come to offer them their first tastes they will already be comfortable in the environment. It also gives you a great opportunity to see how steady and stable they are when sat in their chair.

Check out sign language – using sign with your baby is an amazing skill to expose them to. It's a precursor to verbal language and builds communication skills, it also alleviates frustration for your baby when they are able to communicate their needs and it is a great companion to weaning! Search your native sign language or Makaton and choose a few signs you can use during mealtimes. We started with 'eat', 'water', 'all done' and 'more'. For the first few months, you will just be performing the signs to them (alongside saying the words and linking it to a behaviour, such as signing and saying 'all done' every time you take their plate away). But over time they will start signing back and they will enjoy being able to tell you what they want! We started sign with Rue when she was 7 months old, but you can start much sooner (from birth if you like!). I was signing at her for the first few months, then when Rue was around 10 months she started to sign back when prompted (I asked her if she was all done, and she would do the sign). From 11 months she was signing independently without me prompting her. Even though she's now starting to talk, she will still use signs today, such as eat and more, so it remains a helpful skill throughout their early years.

Things to research and read up on:

▶ If you've read the Crash Course section of this book, you'll be pretty clued up by now! Some key sections for early weaning are the three signs of readiness (page 20), allergens (page 42) and gagging vs. choking (page 30).

▶ Baby first aid (sja.org.uk/moonandrue).

▶ Dairy, egg and wheat alternatives – just in case your little one does react to one of the big three, it's helpful to know what options you could turn to instead!

▶ How to serve foods safely (NHS website, Solid Starts website, First Steps Nutrition Website).

Stock the cupboards

Although you might not know exactly what meals you will be serving yet, you can begin to build up your cupboard staples so you have lots of foods and flavours to fall back on. These ingredients are all great options as they have a long shelf-life and will come in handy once you're up and running!

Rolled oats or instant oats (regular rolled oats are fine from 6 months old)	Rice	Cumin	**Reduced-sugar/-salt baked beans**
	Chopped tomatoes	**Mild curry powder**	**Peanut butter** (no added sugar)
Plain and **self-raising flour**	**Full-fat coconut milk**	Basil	**Tree nut butters**, such as almond or cashew (no added sugar)
	Tomato purée	Oregano	
Baking powder and **bicarbonate of soda**	Passata	**Onion granules**	
	Hemp seeds	**Garlic granules/powder**	
Kidney beans	**Chia seeds**		
Cannellini beans	**Ground flaxseed**	**Baby friendly stock** (very low salt – e.g. Piccolo, Kallo or Knoor)	
Split red lentils	**Desiccated coconut**		
Pasta (fusilloni or fusilli is a great starter shape)	Cinnamon	**Frozen broccoli, peas and/or mixed veg**	
	Smoked paprika		
	Garam masala		

Now onto the recipes, split by the age and stage of your baby. These are followed by a first month of weaning meal plan and more weekly meal plans to use later into your weaning journey. Enjoy!

Early Days (6–7 months)

Breakfasts

Lunches

Dinners

On the Go

Illness/Teething

Breakfasts

Lunches

Dinners

On the Go

Illness/Teething

STAGE

1

Stage 1: Early Days (6–7 months)

At last, it's time to start! Bibs, cloths and mops at the ready, for many of these first meals it will feel like more food ends up on the highchair, floor or your baby's face than in your baby's tummy. It's all part of the fun, and remember that it's their whole experience of the food that counts – seeing it, touching it, smelling it, hearing you talk about it and tasting it (...some of it, at least).

Start off gently with some simple first tastes; they won't need much on their plate and you don't want to overwhelm them. Two or three pieces of food is more than enough, keeping in mind to space out allergens. Try to make their first experience of food an earthy vegetable, like broccoli, cauliflower or very soft green beans. Babies are born with an innate love of sweet foods already, so don't start with something sweet. If your baby cries during any of their meals, this is usually just down to feeling overwhelmed. Give them lots of cuddles and try again when you can.

The first 'meal' I served Rue was an adult finger-sized piece of roasted sweet potato, a spear of roasted courgette and a little houmous on the side. I preloaded a weaning spoon with some houmous, which she quite enjoyed slobbering all over. She then jumped in with her hands and the remainder of the houmous (which had only been a tablespoon to start with) seemed to multiply before my very eyes as she spread endless amounts of it across her face, highchair tray and up her sleeves. She pulled a look of abject disgust at her sweet potato (now one of her favourite foods) and gagged the second it was in her mouth. Then she rounded off the meal by gumming the flesh of the courgette for a good 5 minutes. In the world of weaning, that meal was a great success, despite very little of it reaching her tummy.

Your baby might throw themselves in headfirst (literally), or hardly touch a thing in front of them, but each of these food exposures is teaching them a lot. Don't be put off if things don't go to plan – they are at the very beginning of this learning journey and have every future meal of their life to come!

Skills

- Palmar grasp – Your baby will be using their palmar grasp at this stage – holding food in their fist. Serve foods in pieces the size of an adult finger.

- Cutlery – Have their cutlery present at mealtimes, even though it will mostly be a passive participant. You can preload foods that will stay on the spoon easily (such as yoghurt) and hand it to them. But mostly it's fine to leave them to explore with their hands.

- Open cup – Introduce an open cup to give your baby sips of water alongside solids meals. You will need to hold and tip the cup for them until around 12 months. You can also offer a free-flowing cup with a lid to give your baby independent practice of holding the cup and tipping it. You can progress to removing the lid when you think they are ready.

Top tips

- Bring a damp cloth to the table with you. This is not to clean your baby mid-meal, as this would be pointless and potentially off-putting for them, but to catch any spills – food on the table or on your hands while you help them, and on your clothes. While we're on the subject, don't wear your Sunday best, as sometimes you can end up almost as messy as them!

- Open plates are often easier to navigate at this age.

- To reduce waste, store any leftovers to be reused. Cooked vegetables can be frozen to use in future or to throw into soups, stews and curries.

- Practise some signs at mealtime with your baby. 'Eat', 'more', 'all done' and 'water' are great mealtime signs to introduce them to.

What to expect

- Facial expressions galore! Remember, looks of disgust, shudders and gagging don't indicate they don't like something, so don't take these as a sign to stop offering that food.

- Lots of gagging. If you find this difficult, try to remind yourself that gagging is a good thing and the only way past this phase is more eating practice.

- If your baby doesn't seem to want to engage, strip things right back with just one piece of food at a time. Eat alongside them, make it look great and try not to put any pressure on yourself or them – they will get there.

- Sometimes your baby will pick things up from their plate, but it's also okay to hand them food items as well. Just be sure your baby is showing the sign of readiness and can lift food to their own mouth.

The recipes throughout the book will all have dietary notes, as such:

V = Vegan

VG = Vegetarian

GF = Gluten-free

DF = Dairy-free

NF = Nut-free

Porridge Fingers

5 mins   5 mins

VG   NF

Makes 6–8 porridge fingers

60g porridge oats
180ml milk of choice*
1 banana
2 strawberries, hulled

Full-fat yoghurt, to serve

*If using a milk substitute, I'd recommend unsweetened fortified oat milk

Fridge: up to 3 days
Freezer: up to 3 months
Freezing method: flash freeze (Pop the food pieces on a tray or plate with gaps between each and freeze them for 2 hours before transferring the pieces to a freezer bag or tub.)

There's nothing quite like the goodness of porridge, but when it comes to self-feeding it's not the most ideal food. Glue-like oats make for fantastic sensory play, but when you're desperately wiping them from every crevice imaginable morning after morning, it can wear a bit thin! These porridge fingers are a great alternative, especially in the early days of weaning, as they're easy for your baby to hold without any need for cutlery. They can also be made with a non-dairy milk if you've not yet introduced dairy as an allergen.

1. Spread the oats evenly across the base of a small microwaveable dish or tupperware box, roughly 10cm x 20cm and 4cm deep, then pour over the milk.

2. In another bowl, mash together the banana and strawberries.

3. Add the fruit mixture to the oats and milk and mix it all together.

4. Pop the box into the microwave on High for 2 minutes 30 seconds – when it comes out you'll notice that the mixture is still wet, particularly in the centre, so continue to microwave it at 30-second intervals until you can touch the back of a fork to the top of the mixture and it comes away clean.

5. Leave the mixture in the dish to cool and solidify, then run a knife around the edge of the dish, upturn it and give it a gentle wiggle to shake free the whole porridge block.

6. Cut into finger slices and serve on their own or with some full-fat yoghurt, if you like.

What's good:

Iron-rich: fortified oats.

Potassium-rich: strawberries and banana.

Ideal for palmar grip: easy self-feeding.

Low-Allergen Pancakes

To be honest, if I read 'no gluten, no egg, no dairy' on a menu I'd likely be thinking 'no fun'. Luckily, that's not the case at all with these little delights. This is a super-easy pancake batter that is perfect for breakfasts and on-the-go weaning. All you need to do is throw the ingredients into a blender, which means minimal washing-up too! You're welcome.

5 mins   10 mins

V   VG   DF   GF*   NF

Makes 8–10 mini pancakes

50g porridge oats*
1 banana
Splash of vegetable oil
50ml unsweetened fortified
    oat milk

1 tbsp plain coconut yoghurt
    and some squished
    blueberries, to serve

*Although oats do not contain gluten they can be manufactured with gluten-containing foods. So buy oats labelled as 'gluten-free' if your baby is intolerant of gluten.

Fridge: up to 3 days
Freezer: up to 3 months
Freezing method: freezer
    bag, separate pancakes
    with baking paper

1. Blitz the oats in a blender until they are a fine, flour-like texture.

2. Add the rest of the ingredients and blend to a smooth batter. It should be thick but pourable – a custard-like consistency. Add more milk if you need to, but you don't want the batter to be too thin.

3. Heat a non-stick pan over a medium heat. Ladle in some batter to form pancakes of around 4cm in diameter – you may need to cook these in batches.

4. Cook for 2–3 minutes until bubbles begin to appear, then flip the pancakes and cook for a further minute on the other side. Repeat with all the batter.

5. Serve with a tablespoon of coconut yoghurt and some squished blueberries.

Tips: Add a sprinkle of ground cinnamon and a handful of grated apple (or even carrot or courgette!) to hide even more goodness in this meal.

What's good: Allergy friendly: great for early weaning before allergens have been introduced.

Oats: gentle on digestion and rich in nutrients.

Chia Jam on Toast

5 mins   10 mins

V   VG   DF   NF

Makes 6–8 portions of jam*

150g fresh or frozen
    strawberries
100g fresh or frozen blueberries
Squeeze of lemon juice
1 tsp vanilla extract
1 tsp ground cinnamon
1 tbsp chia seeds
Bread of choice

Unsalted butter (or dairy-free
    alternative), for spreading

*1 portion = a few
    tablespoons, enough to
    have in the fridge and use
    through the week

Fridge: airtight jar or tub for
    up to 5 days
Freezer: in portions for up to
    3 months
Freezing method: portions
    for up to 3 months in ice
    cube trays. Defrost in the
    fridge overnight

There is no way to make jam without feeling like a proper little homemaker. It's giving quaint, it's giving twee. You are Snow White, and hundreds of woodland creatures are flocking to serenade you as you humbly stir your jam. Embrace it! Enjoy it!

Most traditional jams and preserves are around 60 per cent sugar, which is far too much for little people with developing taste buds and teeth. This recipe is not only baby-friendly, it has the added bonus of chia seeds, which bring with them a great dose of iron, calcium, protein and much more.

As your little one gets older, you might decide to add some sweetness to their jam with a liquid sweetener such as honey. But remember, **never** give honey to under ones. A little cinnamon and vanilla extract will be more than enough, alongside the fruits, to add the subtle sweetness that their taste buds need. Even with no added sugar, remember cooked fruits are still sugary, so offering them in moderation is key!

1. Heat a large saucepan over a medium heat and add the berries, lemon juice, vanilla extract and cinnamon. Cover and cook for 5–10 minutes, stirring occasionally.

2. Remove the pan from the heat. The remainder of the process happens as the jam cools.

3. Use a masher to mash the fruit, breaking down any large lumps as much as possible.

4. Add the chia seeds and combine well, then set aside for 15 minutes. Stir, then leave for another 15 minutes. As the jam cools and the chia seeds bloom you should notice the mixture thicken.

5. Once the jam is cool enough to eat, toast your bread, spread on your butter and top with some of the jam.

6. Leave the remaining jam to cool completely before portioning into jars, tubs and ice cube trays to use another day on toast or as a yummy yoghurt or breakfast porridge topper (see page 93).

What's good:

Chia seeds: iron, calcium, protein and omega 3s for brain development.

No added sugars: much better for dental health.

Lentil Pasta Sauce

10 mins   30 mins

V   VG   DF   NF   GF

Makes 6–10 portions

150g dried red lentils
1 tsp olive oil
1 courgette, peeled and cut
   into 1cm slices
1 carrot, peeled and cut into
   1cm slices
Dried mixed herbs (basil,
   parsley and oregano all
   work well)
500g passata
500ml baby-friendly
   vegetable stock (0.1g salt
   per 100g) or boiling water

Cooked fusilli, a sprinkle
   of hemp seeds and 1 tsp
   cream cheese (or dairy-
   free alternative), to serve

Fridge: in an airtight
   container for 4 days
Freezer: up to 3 months
Freezing method: ice cube tray

Lentils are a nutritional powerhouse, packed with B vitamins, magnesium, zinc and potassium. They're rich in iron, which is key for a weaning baby, and also a great source of protein. Used as the base for this sauce, they add a subtle earthy flavour, and when combined with tomato, carrot, courgette or any other veggie you like, the end result is a tasty and versatile pasta sauce.

Also, one day you might find yourself in the depths of toddler fussy-eating hell. Pasta in tomato sauce seems to be one of the few things deemed acceptable during this phase, so having this nutrient-rich option in your back pocket is never going to be a bad thing!

1. Put your lentils in a sieve and give them a thorough rinse.

2. Add the olive oil to a large pan and pop in your veg, then add the rinsed lentils, herbs, passata and stock and stir well.

3. Bring to a gentle boil, then cover and cook for 20–30 minutes, stirring occasionally, until the lentils and veg are soft.

4. Use a hand blender (or transfer it to a traditional blender) and whizz the sauce to your desired texture.

5. This is a high-fibre sauce, so your little one will only need 1–3 tablespoons of sauce per serving. Mix with cooked fusilli and a little sprinkle of hemp seeds for added grip. You can also mix 1 teaspoon of cream cheese (or dairy-free alternative) into the sauce before serving for a thicker, more velvety texture with some added fats.

What's good:

Messy meal: great sensory play.

Courgette: rich in vitamin C, beta-carotene and antioxidants for eye health.

Homemade Houmous with Dippers

5 mins

Makes around 250g of houmous

50g tahini
100g tinned chickpeas
    (drained weight), rinsed
2 tbsp olive oil
Juice of ½ lemon
1 garlic clove, crushed**

For dippers:
Roasted or steamed batons/
    slices of carrot, courgette,
    sweet potato or red pepper
Toast soldiers
Homemade flatbread (see
    page 156)

*Depending on bread used

**You might want to add half of your garlic first and then taste test, depending on how garlicky you want it to be! If the garlic is too much, adding some more lemon juice should balance out the taste.

Houmous is a great baby food. An iron-rich chickpea base, offering lots of protein and fibre, mixed with tahini which keeps up exposure to sesame (a top allergen). Not only does homemade houmous taste better, it also gives you control of the quality of the oils used and the levels of salt and sugar that have been added, as both of these factors can vary with store-bought options.

Houmous is also super versatile. It's a texture that babies love and it can be added to meals as a dip, a spread or be the star of the show, as it is here. It also makes a great toast topper (see page 76), pasta sauce (see page 127) and can even be spread on puff pastry and rolled up to make houmous pinwheels. For serving to adults, simply add salt to taste and enjoy!

1. Add all the houmous ingredients to a blender and whizz to combine.

2. Once blended, check the consistency. Add some warm water in tiny amounts until you feel it is a consistency you are happy with. I would aim for a runnier houmous for younger babies.

3. Serve the houmous in a bowl or in the centre of a plate with the veggie or bread dippers ready to be dipped!

For tasty variations on the classic houmous, try adding:

- ½ onion, chopped
- 1 roasted red pepper, roughly chopped
- 2 tbsp pesto
- 1 tsp smoked paprika
- 50g microwave-steamed sweet potato cubes

Fridge: in an airtight container for up to 4 days
Freezer: up to 4 months, but ideally eat within 2 months
Freezing method: in small portions in tubs or freezer bags. To defrost, transfer to the fridge for a few hours or, ideally, overnight

Tips:

Rinsing chickpeas in cold water reduces the salt content and also makes them easier to digest.

Adding a thin layer of olive oil can help the houmous retain moisture during freezing and thawing.

What's good:

Tahini: calcium and sesame exposure.

Chickpeas: iron, plant-based protein and fibre.

Olive oil: a healthy fat, rich in antioxidants.

No-Egg Broccoli Tots

15 mins   15 mins

VG   NF

Makes 8 tots

100g frozen or raw broccoli
    florets
100g frozen or raw carrots,
    roughly chopped
50g cheese, grated
2 tsp dried oregano
1 tsp olive oil
¼ tsp onion granules
50g breadcrumbs (1 slice of
    bread, blended into crumbs)

Fridge: 4 days
Freezer: up to 2 months
Freezing method: flash
    freeze, then transfer to
    a freezer bag

What's good: Broccoli: rich in iron and vitamin C.

Carrot: rich in beta carotene and vitamin B6, which is important for brain development.

No egg: a great lunch option if you haven't yet introduced egg as an allergen.

Very easy to whip up, these tots are a great less-mess lunch option that are full of flavour. For younger babies, one or two tots, cut in half lengthways to expose the soft insides, is a perfect complete meal. For older weaners and children, a few tots with some dipping sauce always goes down a storm! The ingredients here will give you 8 tots, but it's easy to scale up and make more if you want to build a freezer stash.

1. Microwave-steam your broccoli and carrots in a covered microwaveable dish with 2 tablespoons of water for 4–5 minutes, stirring halfway. Leave to cool.

2. Using a food processor, masher or knife, finely chop your cooked broccoli and carrots.

3. In a large mixing bowl, add the veggies, cheese, oregano, olive oil and onion granules. Give this all a good stir to ensure the seasonings are evenly spread throughout.

4. Add around half your breadcrumbs and stir them in. Do the remainder of the mixing by hand, adding the rest of your breadcrumbs bit by bit until the mixture starts to hold together when you squeeze it.

5. Squeeze all of the mixture together in one lump, then split it into 8 equal portions.

6. Take each portion and squeeze it into little log shapes to make your tots. Aim to keep all of your tots at a uniform depth so that they cook evenly.

7. These can be cooked in the oven, air fryer or pan. If cooking in the oven, cook at 200°C (180°C fan) for around 12 minutes, turning halfway; in the air fryer, cook at 180°C for 10 minutes, turning halfway; or fry in a pan over a medium heat with some olive oil for around 3 minutes on each side. As all of the ingredients in these tots are technically already 'cooked', it doesn't really matter how long you leave them in the oven/air fryer/pan. It's better to just keep in mind what you feel your baby can cope with in terms of crispness. Pan-cooking might result in a crispier outer coating, but it's also easier to burn the outsides with this method, so it might be preferable to use one of the other methods in the early stages of weaning.

Veggie Curry

15 mins   35 mins

V   VG   DF*   NF   GF*

Makes 6–8 baby portions, or 2 adult portions and 2 baby portions

1 x 215g tin of kidney beans (approx. 130g drained weight), rinsed
½ butternut squash, peeled and chopped into chunks
1 tbsp olive oil
1 garlic clove
2 tomatoes, chopped
2 tbsp mild curry powder
1 tbsp ground cumin
500ml baby-friendly vegetable stock

1 tbsp plain yoghurt (or a dairy-free alternative), to serve (optional)
Rice, homemade flatbread (page 156), to serve

*Depending on stock and bread used.

Fridge: up to 3 days
Freezer: up to 3 months
Freezing method: portion into freezer bags

This is a lovely little first curry to start introducing your baby to more complex flavour profiles. Babies love flavour, so don't be afraid to add subtle spices when cooking for them! This is definitely another take-deep-breaths meal if you aren't a great fan of mess, so get them in a good cover-up or make it a before-bath meal. Pre-load some spoonfuls for them to introduce them to cutlery, but remember, eating with their hands is fine. The benefits to messy meals are huge; not only is it a rich, exploratory, sensory experience, it also boosts fine motor skills and has even been linked to early language development.

1. Chop or mash the kidney beans.* I chop mine into quarters, which takes a little longer than mashing but I personally prefer the texture.

2. Add your chunks of squash to a pan over a medium heat with the olive oil, then add your garlic, chopped tomatoes and the kidney beans. Sprinkle over the spices and stir well, allowing these flavours to cook through for a few minutes.

3. Pour over the stock and bring to a gentle bubble while stirring. Cook, uncovered, for 30 minutes to reduce.

4. For a creamier curry, mix 1 tablespoon of yoghurt (or a dairy-free alternative) into the curry before serving. Serve with rice, homemade flatbread, or on its own.

*As this is early in the weaning journey, I still prefer to chop or mash beans at this stage. You can mash them post-cooking more easily, if you like. Beans do become soft and mushy during cooking, though, so once your baby has had more chewing practice it isn't necessary to mash them.

Tip: To make peeling and chopping easier, slice the top and bottom off your squash and microwave it whole for around 3 minutes to soften the squash (just remember to allow it to cool a bit before handling!).

What's good: Curry powder: new flavours and rich in anti-inflammatory compounds such as curcumin.

Messy meal: great for sensory learning, fine motor development and oral motor development.

Mediterranean Chicken

15 mins   30+ mins   1 hour

DF   NF   GF*

This is a yummy dish for the whole family, and it couldn't be easier to make, with everything cooking together in one roasting dish. The only thing this recipe needs is time – allow the chicken to marinate in the spices to soak up the flavours, then give it plenty of time to roast slowly in the oven. Chicken, vegetables and potatoes all cooked in the subtle spices provides a complete meal packed with nutrients, with lots of textures and tastes for your baby to explore!

Makes 2 adult portions and 4 baby portions

1 tbsp olive oil, plus extra for cooking
2 tbsp lemon juice
1 garlic clove or 1 tsp garlic granules
1 tsp smoked paprika
2 tsp dried oregano
600–700g skinless and boneless chicken thighs
5 or 6 potatoes (Maris Pipers), peeled and each cut into 8 wedges
1 large red onion, chopped
300ml baby-friendly chicken stock
1 courgette, chopped

*check stock

Fridge: 2 days
Freezer: up to 3 months
Freezing method: portion into freezer bags. To defrost, transfer to the fridge overnight

1. In a large mixing bowl, combine the olive oil, lemon juice, garlic, paprika and oregano.

2. Use a knife to slit the surface of each chicken thigh a few times, then add them to the bowl with the marinade. Stir everything well, cover and refrigerate for at least 30 minutes – or marinate overnight for best results.

3. When you are ready to cook, preheat the oven to 180°C (160°C fan).

4. In a large roasting dish, add a splash of olive oil, then tip in the potatoes and onion.

5. Lift the chicken thighs out of the marinade and place on top of the veggies. Put the remaining marinade to one side.

6. Pour over the chicken stock. The veggies and chicken should be partly in the liquid but the chicken doesn't need to be fully submerged. Cover with foil and cook for 30 minutes.

7. Remove from the oven and take off the foil. Turn your chicken pieces over, add the courgette and gently mix in any vegetables that are around the edge. Pour the remaining marinade over your chicken and return the tray to the oven for a further 30 minutes.

8. When serving, ensure all bits of potato are soft by flattening them with a fork. For 6-month-olds, chicken pieces should be left large (the size of 2 adult fingers). At this younger age, your baby might just suck on the chicken pieces rather than chewing them, but they will still get nutrients by doing this. Once your baby reaches 8 or 9 months, you can shred the chicken into small chunks.

What's good:

Dark meat: richer in nutrients such as iron, zinc and selenium.

Red onion and potatoes: good source of vitamin B6 for healthy metabolism.

First Fish and Chips

15 mins   20 mins

Makes 2 baby portions

¼ baking potato, cut into
  chunky chip shapes
½ white fish fillet, such as
  haddock or cod (fresh or
  frozen)
1 tsp vegetable oil
Sprinkle of garlic powder
  and/or onion powder
30g frozen peas
A splash of milk
A squeeze of lemon juice

A fun little twist on an adult favourite. If you keep a stash of frozen fish in the freezer, this meal is ideal to fall back on for something nutritious and easy to eat. There's no batter here (criminal, I know), but as your little one gets older, rolling the fish in some egg and then breadcrumbs before cooking makes the perfect crispy coating. Finned fish is an allergen, so keep earlier portions small and watch your baby for any reactions.

1. Preheat the oven to 200°C (180°C fan).

2. Put the potatoes in a microwaveable dish and cover loosely with some kitchen roll. Microwave on High for 4 minutes until they begin to soften.

3. Feel your fish to check for any small bones (if using frozen fish, you'll need to check it once cooked). Wrap in foil and place the fish and the potato onto a baking tray. In a small bowl, mix the oil with the garlic and/or onion powder. Lightly brush this mixture over the chips. Bake for 15–20 minutes, turning the chips over at regular intervals.

4. Boil the peas in a pan of boiling water for 5 minutes and then strain. Add the peas back to the pan and add in the milk and lemon juice and use a hand blender to blitz until mushy.

5. Remove the fish and potato from the oven. The fish should be opaque and flaky, while the potato should be slightly crispy on the outside (although not as crispy as us adults might like!) and soft/easy to smush between forefinger and thumb.

6. Plate up your fish and chips with the pea mixture.

What's good: White fish: rich in protein and haem iron and promotes strong bones; flaky in texture and easy for baby to chew.

Toast – Eight Ways

Toast is a weaning parent's best friend. Quick and easy, it's an ideal meal to fall back on when you're just not sure what to offer. Toast and unsalted butter is, of course, fine, but you might have some toast-induced guilt if you resort to offering that combination day in, day out. There are easy ways to turn the toast into a fully nutritious meal, and in the long run it's beneficial to offer a variety of toppings. It can be easy for children to get very fixed ideas about their meals, especially when the 'fussy' phases rear their head. The more variety you offer from day one, the less narrow their minds will be in future. I'm not suggesting you frenziedly offer all of these ideas on a loop, but rather have a few favourites that you can whip out of your back pocket when you want to mix things up a bit!

1. Eggs (VG NF)

There are so many ways to offer this simple meal! In the early stages, a little bit of hard-boiled egg, mashed with a dash of your milk of choice, makes a great puréed topping. As time progresses, scrambled egg on toast is an easy and nutritious meal. And, of course, softly-boiled egg* with soldiers to dip! Rue had seen me eat this many times and I was surprised at how quickly she picked up the technique herself – she knew what to do straight away and to this day a 'dip-dip egg' is one of our favourite go-tos when we're pushed for time. Egg is a top allergen, so try to include a bit of white and yolk in each serving. It's also a good idea to serve egg alongside something rich in vitamin C, like pepper or fruit, as eggs don't contain any vitamin C themselves.

2. Cream Cheese and Raspberries (VG NF)

Strawberries also work well here, but I like to use raspberries as they break down so easily (you don't even need to cut or mash them beforehand). Simply spread your cream cheese onto the toast, add 1 or 2 raspberries on top and use your knife to press them into the cheese. Sprinkle over some hemp seeds for a boost of protein.

3. Avocado and Hemp Seeds (V VG NF DF)

Mashed avocado on toast – a hipster's dream. Top with a generous sprinkle of hemp seeds for a boost of protein, and you can even experiment with a tiny squeeze of lemon juice to introduce a subtle sour taste.

4. Houmous (V VG NF DF)

This is a great, less-messy way to give your little one houmous. Chickpeas provide a healthy dose of protein, and houmous also keeps up exposures to sesame which is a top allergen. See page 66 for some flavour twist variations.

*Eggs stamped with the British Red Lion logo are safe to be served soft-boiled, as the hens that lay them are vaccinated against salmonella. I find cooking for 4½–5 minutes (in water that's bubbling energetically) gives the perfect dipping yolk.

5. Tahini and Cinnamon (V VG NF DF)

Tahini is a great alternative to nut butters and is used in many desserts in Middle Eastern cooking. It also provides a good amount of protein and key minerals, and keeps up exposures to sesame. Mix in a sprinkle of ground cinnamon and add a thin layer to buttered toast. You can also add some grated apple or pear on top to finish.

6. Chia Jam (V VG NF DF)

No, you're not getting deja-vu, I did share this option a few pages ago in the breakfast section. But the flavours don't stop at strawberry and blueberry. Apples, pears, plums, blackberries, cherries and even more tropical fruits like mango can be made into delicious jams for toast (sticking to the same overall fruit measurements in the recipe on page 62). Chia seeds add a boost of protein, calcium and omega 3s, so they are ideal for a growing body and brain.

7. Another Nut Butter (V VG DF)

Don't forget to include tree nuts in your little one's diet, as these are a separate allergen category to peanuts. Almond, hazelnut and cashew butter are great options here and always work nicely either alone or paired with a fruit such as banana, grated apple or pear, or chopped blueberries or strawberries.

8. Banana and Peanut Butter (V VG DF)

Opt for a super-thin layer of peanut butter – to avoid any clagginess – followed by a layer of mashed or thinly sliced banana. Not only is it important to keep up peanut butter exposure, it's also a good source of protein, and pairing it with banana is a classic flavour combo.

Savoury Muffins

15 mins   25 mins

VG   NF

Makes 12 muffins

150g frozen peas
120ml milk
120g plain flour
1 tsp baking powder
½ tsp garlic granules
50g cheese, grated
1 spring onion, finely chopped
1 egg
40ml olive or vegetable oil

Fridge: 3 days
Freezer: up to 3 months
Freezing method: freezer bag

In the early days of weaning, it can sometimes feel like you are tied down to staying in the house. The majority of restaurant food just isn't suitable for a little one at the very beginning of the weaning journey, and planning food that you can take out and about with you can feel like a challenge. These muffins were a lifesaver to me during that time! I tried to make sure I always had a batch cooked. They freeze and defrost really well, have a good dose of veggies and are an easy self-feeding option that's relatively mess-free. Any vegetables work well here. We love the pea and spring onion flavour in these but they can also be made with grated carrot or sweet potato, cooked broccoli or cauliflower, and even salad vegetables like peppers and tomatoes.

1. Preheat the oven to 190°C (170°C fan). Place 12 muffin cases into a 12-hole muffin tin.

2. Cook the peas in a pan of boiling water, then drain and blend to a purée with a splash of the milk.

3. In a large mixing bowl, combine the pea mix with the flour, baking powder, garlic granules, cheese and spring onion.

4. In a second bowl, add the remaining milk, the egg and oil. Whisk together to break down the egg yolk.

5. Pour the wet ingredients into the dry ingredients and stir everything together well to make a thickish batter. Divide the batter equally among the muffin cases then cook for 25 minutes, until a skewer inserted into the centre of one muffin comes out clean.

6. At 6 months old, serve one muffin cut in half to expose the soft insides. At 8–9 months, serve whole muffins or cut them into chunks for pincer-grip practice.

What's good:

Muffins: easy self-feeding and a perfect grab-and-go option.

Peas: rich in vitamin C to aid iron absorption.

Veggie Scramble

10 mins   4 mins

VG   NF   GF

Makes 1–2 baby portions

Olive oil or unsalted butter,
   for frying
2–3 cherry tomatoes, seeds
   removed and finely chopped
¼ red pepper, finely chopped
1 egg
A handful of grated cheese
A sprinkle of dried oregano
A splash of milk (optional)

Squished blueberries, some
   buttered tiger loaf and
   Tropical Yoghurt Bark
   (page 112), to serve

Fridge: 3 days
Freezer: up to 3 months
Freezing method: wrap in
   cling film and pop in a
   freezer bag

This was a go-to meal for us during teething or illness, because it's super nutritious while being soft and forgiving for sore little gums! On top of that, if they do refuse the meal (which is very common during teething or feeling unwell), it can be stored in the fridge and reheated, so nothing needs to go to waste. You can throw in any veggies, but tomato and red pepper add their own distinct flavours that work really well, alongside a good boost of vitamin C.

1. Heat a small pan over a medium heat with some olive oil or unsalted butter.

2. Throw in your veggies and cook, stirring regularly, until they have softened. Remove any large or peeling pieces of pepper or tomato skin that you notice.

3. In a bowl, crack your egg, then add the cheese and oregano and whisk. You can also add a small splash of milk, if you like.

4. Add the egg mixture to the pan, covering the veggies. Leave for a minute before stirring to 'scramble'. Move the egg around the pan until it is cooked.

5. Serve with squished blueberries and some buttered tiger loaf, if you like. You could also follow it up with some frozen tropical yoghurt bark (page 112) made with fruit puree.

What's good:

Soft texture: for sore gums.

Red pepper: rich in immune system boosters such as vitamin C and beta-carotene.

Starting to Click (8–9 months)

Breakfasts

Lunches

Dinners

On the Go

Illness/Teething

STAGE 2

Stage 2: Starting to Click (8–9 months)

This was the period of time where I really started to notice Rue taking more ownership of her meals. She seemed comfortable with the familiarity of mealtimes and got stuck into whatever I was serving. Rue is a foodie, so don't worry if your baby is not quite there yet, but what you should notice is that they're used to the mealtime routine – they know what's about to go down when the bib goes on! There will hopefully be a little less gagging (although it will still be a regular feature) and a little more eaten (although don't be disheartened if they're not clearing their plate). You will have worked your way through many allergens by now, so remember to keep including foods such as nut butters in their diet to maintain regular exposures.

One curveball that babies do like throwing around at this time is dropping food from their highchair. If your child is like mine, this will be accompanied by looking you dead in the eyes with an expressionless stare as they silently hold their food over the side of the tray, before dropping it onto the floor below with a thud. It is a mixture of them feeling more comfortable at mealtimes, experimenting with object permanence, testing boundaries and testing your reactions. Try not to burst out laughing... we're only human, so you might fail at this a few times (I know I did!), but it's really important not to overreact as this can create a situation where they continue doing it for longer.

Skills

- Pincer grip – By this age your baby is developing the ability to pick up food between their forefinger and thumb. Continue to offer adult finger-sized slices of food alongside some cut into smaller chunks. Squished blueberries make for fantastic pincer grip practice.

- Cutlery – Continue to preload cutlery and hand it to them at different points throughout a meal.

- Straw cup – You could introduce a straw cup at this stage as a new skill. Rotate open cups and straw cups for practice of both drinking methods. Look up the 'pipette method' if your baby is struggling to grasp how to suck from the straw.

What to expect

- Food flinging, food dropping, plate flipping and cutlery being launched across the room like an Olympic javelin. As your baby builds familiarity with mealtimes, they might display some more boisterous behaviours. Try not to overreact and check whether it could be a signal that they are finished with their meal.

- Teething can throw a spanner in the works so if you notice a sudden loss of appetite or interest, there's every chance a tooth is on the way.

Top tips

- Emphasise and encourage the 'all done' sign at mealtimes when you take their plate away, to start to give your baby the tools to communicate that they're finished with a meal.

- Use some good suction plates to reduce the chance of them flipping their plate.

- Serve soft and cooling foods during teething to soothe sore gums.

Sweet Potato Pancakes

15 mins   15 mins

VG

Makes 12 pancakes

500g sweet potato (300g
    steamed), peeled and cut
    into 1cm slices
2 eggs
3 tbsp plain flour
1 tsp baking powder
1 tsp vanilla extract
1 tbsp ground cinnamon
Unsalted butter, for cooking

Steamed apple chunks and
    a drizzle of peanut butter,
    to serve

Fridge: 3 days
Freezer: up to 3 months
Freezing method: freezer
    bag, pancakes separated
    with baking paper

Sweet potatoes are a gift. Not only are these starchy veggies a good source of iron and vitamin C, they can also be disguised in many sweet treats (such as my sweet potato brownies on page 196). There's a reason they are such a fan favourite in weaning – they appeal to a baby's preference for sweet things while sneaking in a lot of goodness. In these pancakes, the cinnamon and vanilla complement the potato perfectly for a light and satisfying breakfast option.

1. Roast or microwave-steam your sweet potato by placing the slices on a microwaveable dish, loosely cover with a sheet of kitchen roll and microwave on High for 7–8 minutes until soft.

2. Mash the softened sweet potato, then add in the eggs and stir to combine. Fold in the flour, baking powder, vanilla extract and cinnamon.

3. Heat a non-stick frying pan over a medium-low heat with a small amount of butter. Use a generous tablespoon of batter per pancake and cook for 2 minutes on each side.

4. Leave to cool on a wire rack before storing/serving.

5. Serve with steamed apple chunks and a drizzle of peanut butter.

What's good:

Sweet potato: aids digestion and rich in vitamin C.

Pancakes: great for grabbing from frozen; defrost in the microwave, toaster or a frying pan.

Baked Veggie Hash Browns

15 mins   25 mins

VG   GF   NF

Makes 4 veggie hash browns

1 small baking potato
½ carrot
½ x 200g tin sweetcorn (no
   added salt), drained
½ tsp onion granules
15g unsalted butter, melted,
   plus more for greasing
50g cheese, grated

Dipping sauce or soft-boiled
   egg, to serve

*Eggs stamped with the
British Red Lion logo are safe
to be served soft-boiled.

Fridge: 2 days
Freezer: these are best fresh
   but can be frozen for up to
   2 months
Freezing method: flash
   freeze, then transfer to a
   freezer bag

These are hash browns with a twist – packed with added veggies and baked instead of fried, which makes them a really suitable and nutritious meal for your little one. These are great at lunch, too, but sometimes it can be nice to mix in savoury options at breakfast. These can be frozen but I personally think they are best eaten fresh – hence the small batch size. If you do want to scale up and freeze the extras, I would recommend reheating in the oven (or an air fryer) to get that delicious, satisfying crispiness back!

1. Preheat the oven to 190°C (170°C fan).

2. Grate the potato and carrot into a clean tea towel, cheesecloth or muslin, then twist together the corners and squeeze out the excess water.

3. Add the drained veggies and sweetcorn to a large mixing bowl. Sprinkle over the onion granules and mix. Add in the melted butter and grated cheese and stir everything together well.

4. Grease 4 holes in a muffin tray with butter. Add 1–2 tablespoons of the hash brown mixture into the greased spaces, then press down gently on each to compact the mixture. Cook for 20–25 minutes, until starting to turn golden on top.

5. Run a knife around the edge of each hash brown before removing them from the tray. Leave to cool on a wire rack.

6. Serve with a dipping sauce or half a softly boiled egg.*

What's good:

Calcium-rich thanks to potatoes, butter and cheese.

A savoury breakfast option to offer variety at mealtimes.

Porridge – Eight Ways

Porridge is a fantastic breakfast for babies. It has an easy to manage texture, a mild and appealing flavour and provides an opportunity for spoon practice. Fortified with iron, oats are high in antioxidants, full of fibre and are a rich energy source – they make the perfect breakfast no matter your age. Don't bother buying anything marketed as 'baby porridge'; not only is the concept totally unnecessary (and not cost-efficient), these products also contain high levels of added fruit concentrates, making them high in sugar.

Cow's milk is fine in porridge, even for babies younger than 12 months, but you can use a milk alternative if your baby has shown an intolerance to dairy. For the perfect porridge for little ones, I like to follow a ratio of 1:3 oats and milk, then microwave on High for 45 seconds. You can, of course, cook it on the hob, I just find the microwave to be the most time-efficient way for those weekday mornings where you need to get going! Make sure to stir it well and check the temperature if you cook it in the microwave, to avoid any hot spots. I've included a table below as a guideline for portion sizes, but take the lead from your little one. Some 7-month-olds will easily gobble up a 30g bowl of porridge (I know, because mine did!) so just adjust portion sizes to suit your child.

Oats + Milk of choice

6 months = 15g + 45ml

7 months = 20g + 60ml

9 months = 30g + 90ml

If you ever feel guilt about repetitive breakfasts – don't! It's realistic that we have similar breakfasts most days, and with porridge there are lots of ways to introduce variety with the toppings you choose. Here are some ideas for you to try when you want to mix things up a bit:

1. Blueberries and Peanut Butter (VG GF)

Use fresh or frozen blueberries and add them to your porridge before cooking, so they cook together. Finish with a drizzle of peanut butter.

2. Peaches and Cream (VG GF NF)

This one sounds like it shouldn't be allowed but it is oh-so good! Add 1 teaspoon of double cream to the porridge before cooking, then add some chopped, fresh, juicy peach to the finished product and mix well. Delicious!

3. Apple and Cinnamon (VG GF NF)

Make your porridge and top with ¼ of an apple, grated. Stir in well, sprinkle over some cinnamon, then serve!

4. Banana and Almond Butter (VG GF)

Make your porridge. Slice half a banana and place it on top, or mash it and mix through. Finish with a sprinkle of hemp seeds and a drizzle of almond butter.

5. Chocolate and Strawberries (VG GF NF)

Mix ½ teaspoon of unsweetened cacao powder into your porridge before cooking. Finish with some chopped strawberries or a drizzle of hazelnut butter!

6. Pineapple and Coconut (VG GF NF)

A little exotic twist on your morning porridge! Finely chop around 1 tablespoon of pineapple, stir it through the porridge, then sprinkle some desiccated coconut on top and add a drizzle of hazelnut butter!

7. Vanilla Poached Pears (VG GF NF)

Prepare and store enough pear to use across breakfasts through the week (around 2 medium-sized per week). In a pan, melt 10g of unsalted butter. Peel and slice your pears and add them to the pan. Add in 1 teaspoon of vanilla extract and cook until the pears soften. Serve mixed through the cooked porridge.

8. Chia Jam (VG GF NF)

Do I ever stop going on about chia jam? The answer is, of course, no. Make your porridge and pop a teaspoon of chia jam on top or mix it through (page 62).

Kidney Bean Burgers

15 mins   15 mins

VG   NF

Makes 4-6 burgers

Olive oil, for frying
1 x 215g tin of kidney beans
    (130g drained weight), rinsed
1 small carrot, grated
20g grated cheese
½ tsp garlic granules
½ tsp smoked paprika
A crack of black pepper
2 tbsp plain flour
Around ¼–½ of 1 beaten egg

Flour, for dusting (optional)

Greek yoghurt and fruit, to
    serve

*If you're really pushed for
time, you can skip this step,
but your beans will be harder
to mash!

Fridge: 3 days
Freezer: up to 3 months
Freezing method: flash
    freeze, then transfer
    to a freezer bag

If kidney beans were on a dating app, their bio would read something along the lines of: not exciting, but dependable. Everyone needs a resident tin of them gathering dust at the back of their cupboard, ready to be called into action when you find yourself at a loose end. Full of plant-based protein and folate, they can be relied upon to bulk up so many different meals. If you find yourself short for time, these bean burgers are an amazing way to put the beans to good use and make baby (and you!) a tasty lunch.

1. Add a small drizzle of oil to a pan over a low heat. Add in your kidney beans and carrot and cook through for 5 minutes, stirring occasionally.*

2. Transfer the beans and carrots to a bowl (leave your pan out for later). Mash the beans and carrots together with the cheese and seasonings plus 2 tablespoons of flour.

3. In a separate bowl, crack an egg and beat it. Add the egg bit by bit to your bean mixture, only using as much as you need. You want it to bind together but not be overly gloopy.

4. Shape into burgers, keeping them all around 1cm thick. Lightly flouring your hands might help if you're finding the mixture sticky.

5. Add your burgers back into your pan over a medium heat, and cook for 4 minutes on each side.

6. Serve with Greek yoghurt (it also doubles up as a dip!) and some fruit.

What's good:

Kidney beans: good source of copper to keep the immune system healthy.

Eggs and beans: a protein-rich meal.

Broccoli Omelette

5 mins   6 mins

VG   GF   NF

Makes 2 baby portions

Handful of frozen broccoli
   (around 30g)
1 egg
10g grated cheese
1 tsp olive oil or a knob of
   unsalted butter

Fruit, to serve (optional)

Fridge: 3 days
Freezer: up to 2 months

This meal is an absolute staple in our house as it's nutritious, quick to prep and stores well. I have a bit of an aversion to egg when it's too eggy (don't ask), but the broccoli and cheese in this omelette make it really flavourful and delicious. When Rue was 6–9 months old, an omelette with one egg made two meals. Now that she's older, we use two eggs and double up the other elements, too. I always make more than I need as it keeps in the fridge (or freezer) really well!

1. Put your frozen broccoli into a microwaveable dish with a splash of water and microwave for 3 minutes.

2. Crack the egg into a cup and add the grated cheese.

3. Mash or finely chop the steamed broccoli and stir it into your egg mixture.

4. Heat the olive oil or butter in a pan over a medium-low heat, then add the egg mixture. Move the broccoli around, if needed, to spread it evenly in the omelette.

5. Cook for 2–3 minutes, then flip over and cook for 2–3 minutes on the other side, until lightly golden.

6. Slice into finger slices from 6 months or pincer chunks from 9 months.

7. Serve with fruit or on its own!

What's good:

Broccoli: provides vitamin C to help absorb the iron from the eggs.

Eggs: nutrient-rich, including choline which promotes brain development.

Potato Veggie Tots

15 mins   25 mins

VG   NF

Makes 12-15 tots

100g potato, peeled and grated
100g veggies, chopped
    (broccoli, peas or
    sweetcorn work well)
A handful of chopped chives
30g cheese, grated
1 egg
Any other herbs or seasoning
    (optional)
2 tbsp plain flour
1 slice of bread, blended into
    breadcrumbs

Fridge: 3-4 days
Freezer: up to 3 months
Freezing method: flash
    freeze, then transfer
    to a freezer bag or tub

Tots! A cute little food to feed your cute little human. Turning any food into a tot or bite is a baby-led weaning favourite because they are perfect for self-feeding and a great way to compact multiple ingredients into one meal.

The star ingredient here is the humble potato. Many of life's greatest pleasures originate with the modest spud: crisps, chips, roasties and, of course, these delightful Potato Veggie Tots.

The great thing about potatoes is not only are they inexpensive, they also contain a great amount of both iron and vitamin C. A lot of a potato's iron resides in its skin, which you can leave on for this recipe if you so wish. If you do decide to peel them, opt for an iron-rich veggie, such as broccoli or peas, to give the tots an extra boost of goodness. The chives bring a perfectly mild, oniony flavour, as well as boosting immunity, digestive health and heart health.

1. Preheat the oven to 200°C (180°C fan).

2. Add the grated potato to a clean tea towel, cheesecloth or muslin, then twist together the corners and squeeze out the excess water.

3. In a bowl, throw together the drained potato, veggies, chives, cheese and egg. Add in any other herbs or seasoning you like and give it a good mix.

4. Sift the flour into the mixture and stir to combine.

5. Add around half of the breadcrumbs to your mixture. Put the remainder into a shallow dish for rolling.

6. Roll the veggie mixture into cylindrical tot shapes, about 2.5cm in diameter. Roll each tot in the remaining breadcrumbs to give them a fine coating and place on a baking tray. Pop in the oven and cook for 25 minutes.

7. To serve at 6 months, cut each tot in half lengthways (to expose the soft insides) for easy self-feeding. From 8 months, offer whole tots.

8. Serve with a baby-friendly sauce (like the baby-friendly tomato dip on page 194) to encourage dipping.

What's good:

Potatoes: a good source of iron and vitamin C.

Chives: choline and folate to enhance the immune system.

Salmon Veggie Pancakes

15 mins   10 mins

DF   NF

Makes 4 pancakes

100g frozen peas
100g frozen or tinned
    sweetcorn*
100g tinned or fresh salmon
2 eggs
2 tbsp plain flour
Olive oil

*Look for salt-free sweetcorn
options where possible

Fridge: 2 days
Freezer: up to 3 months
Freezing method: flash
    freeze, then transfer
    to a freezer bag

Salmon is a perfect fish choice for baby-led weaning. Not only is it soft, flaky and low in mercury, it's also a fantastic source of many of the nutrients your baby needs. Tinned salmon is a great option to have in the cupboard and has come to my rescue many times when I'm nearing the end of the week and the fridge is looking bare. It's got a long shelf life, is already cooked and can be thrown into many dishes (or served as it is) at a moment's notice. Most tinned salmon does come with the bones, which is mildly annoying, but large bones are easy enough to remove and smaller bones are soft and will mash down easily as you flake the fish between your fingers. They are also a great source of calcium, so it's more than fine to leave them in!

These salmon veggie pancakes are always a hit. They are a complete meal for your baby, great to serve from 6 months and easily adaptable depending on what veggies you have in the house.

1. If using frozen, add your peas and sweetcorn to a cup and fill it with boiling water. Leave them to sit while you move on to your salmon.

2. If cooking the salmon from fresh, lightly pan-fry or bake your fillet, then break apart into flakes. If using tinned, remove any larger bones and flake the salmon between your forefinger and thumb to gently mash any smaller bones.

3. Drain your peas and sweetcorn and use a hand blender to whizz them to a chunky purée. Alternatively, you can mash them, but I do find blending them helps with the pancake texture.

4. Add your veggies to your salmon, then add your eggs and combine. Sprinkle over the plain flour and give it all a good mix.

5. Heat a frying pan over a medium heat with a splash of olive oil. Use 2–3 tablespoons of batter per pancake to make 10cm diameter rounds and cook them for 2–3 minutes on each side.

6. Transfer to a wire cooling rack. When they initially come out of the pan the pancakes will seem quite soft, but they firm up as they cool.

7. Serve in finger slices for 6 months and pincer chunks from 9 months.

What's good:

Salmon: omega 3s for brain development, excellent source of B vitamins.

Sweetcorn and peas: rich in vitamin C and antioxidants.

Easy Pizzas

15 mins   13 mins

NF

Makes 2 mini pizzas

100g plain flour, plus extra
   for dusting
100g full-fat Greek yoghurt*
1 tsp baking powder

For toppings:
1 tbsp tomato purée
A handful of grated cheese
Any other toppings you like!
   Lots of things work well
   including:
- diced pepper
- diced tomato
- grated courgette
- chopped onion
- pineapple (yes, I'm one of
   those)
- cooked minced meat
- finely chopped cooked
   chicken breast
Dried oregano

*You can also use plain
yoghurt for this dough, but
it can be a little more watery,
so you may need to reduce
the amount slightly

Fridge: up to 4 days
Freezer: par-cooked bases
   or finished pizzas up to 2
   months
Freezing method: flash
   freeze, then transfer to a
   freezer bag or clingfilm

Does this even need any introduction? Pizza is always a firm favourite, but store-bought options are often highly processed, with varying degrees of sugar, salt and not-so-great fats. These little homemade pizzas are so easy to make and require minimal ingredients to create something delicious. They are also a great way to incorporate meat into your baby's diet, if that is something that makes you nervous. Adding ground or finely chopped cooked meats into the topping will get in that key protein and haem iron – let the pizza be your vehicle!

Also, sentimental sidenote, this is a perfect recipe to make with a toddler. Whenever I cook these pizzas, I get a little watery eyed picturing a day when Rue will be helping me roll out the dough and choosing her own toppings. In my imagination it's a very serene scene... the reality will probably be much more chaotic, but I still can't wait!

1. Preheat the oven to 200°C (180°C fan).

2. In a mixing bowl, add the flour, yoghurt and baking powder and mix together by hand until it forms a dough. Try not to over-knead it – once it's binding together, roll it into a ball.

3. Transfer your dough to a lightly floured surface and cut it into two balls. Roll out each base to around 1cm thick, then transfer to a baking sheet and pop the bases in the oven to par-cook for 5 minutes.

4. Once the bases have had their time in the oven, take them out and build your toppings! Dilute 1 tablespoon of tomato purée with a splash of water and spread evenly across the base, then add the cheese and any other toppings you might like, and sprinkle with some oregano.

5. Return the pizzas to the oven for a further 8 minutes.

6. At 6 months, your baby will probably only need half a pizza, cut into slices, with a little fruit on the side.

What's good:

Easy self-feeding: pizza acts as a great carrier for a variety of nutritious toppings.

Fuss-friendly: further down the line, it's a great way to sneak some nutrients into picky eaters!

Spaghetti Bolognese & Garlic Bread

10 mins   1–1½ hrs

NF

Makes 6–8 baby portions, or 4 adult portions and 2 baby portions

500g beef mince (you can also use lamb, pork or turkey)
Olive oil, for frying
2 garlic cloves
1 onion, chopped
1 tbsp tomato purée
1 tsp smoked paprika
2 tins of chopped tomatoes
500ml baby-friendly beef stock (0.1g salt per 100g)
Spaghetti

For adult/older child portions:
Splash of Worcestershire sauce
1–2 tbsp sugar (optional)

For the garlic bread:
1–2 tbsp softened butter
Handful of chopped parsley (dried or fresh)
1 slice of tiger bread

Fridge: up to 4 days
Freezer: up to 3 months
Freezing method: freezer bags or ice cube tray

I feel no shame in telling you that in our house we eat Spaghetti Bolognese every single week, pretty much without fail. It's an ideal comfort food and yet another easy way to get key meat-based nutrients into your baby's diet. The secret to a good Spaghetti Bolognese is time. It is quick to throw together, but for the best results needs a couple of hours in the pan to slow-cook and reduce.

Another joy of Spag Bol? Mess! Take a deep breath and embrace the fact that your baby will manage to get spaghetti in their hair, nostrils and, somehow, between their toes. It won't always be like this, and the cognitive and sensory development that comes with it is 100 per cent worth it. But maybe don't offer this meal if you're in a rush to get out of the house. It's firmly a 'before-bath' dinner and to attempt it any other time would be foolish to say the least.

1. Pop your mince in a large saucepan over a medium heat with a splash of oil and cook until browned.

2. Press the garlic and put a small amount to one side for the garlic bread. Add the onion to the pan with the remainder of your garlic, then add the tomato purée and smoked paprika to the pan and stir everything well.

3. Add the chopped tomatoes and stock. Bring to the boil, then reduce the heat so that the Bolognese is just gently bubbling. Leave for 1½–2 hours, stirring every 15–20 minutes.

4. When your Bolognese has almost reduced (the excess liquid has cooked off), begin to cook your spaghetti according to the instructions on the packet.

5. When your Bolognese is cooked, remove any baby portions before adding a splash of Worcestershire sauce and some sugar to the adult portions (to taste). Serve up as much as you need for your meal, then set aside the rest to cool before storing in the fridge or freezer for another day.

For the Garlic Bread:

1. In a small bowl, mix the softened butter, the reserved garlic and a sprinkle of parsley. Allow the garlic to sit in the butter for a stronger, more infused taste.

2. Toast your bread.

3. Spread the garlic butter onto the toast. Use the knife to remove any obvious chunks of garlic, as they can be a bit zingy when bitten straight into! Serve immediately.

Sweetcorn Fritters

I know I say this about all of these recipes, but these fritters are very, very yummy. Whenever I make them I have grand ideas about having a freezer stash for Rue, when in reality, four out of five times I end up eating a lot of them myself! But I think we can all agree that feeding Mummy is also important, so it's fine, right?

When it comes to sweetcorn, for younger babies I would blend the kernels and then by 9 months just mash them to break down the structure slightly. The kernels are easily chewed and carried down as part of the fritter. These are also a great option for lunches out and about as they can be enjoyed hot or cold, aren't messy and travel really well.

10 mins   10–15 mins

VG   NF

Makes 10 fritters

60g plain flour
100g tinned or frozen
    sweetcorn (no-salt option)
40g grated cheese
1 spring onion, finely chopped
1 tsp dried oregano
2 eggs
Olive oil, for frying

Tomato Dip (page 194), to serve

Fridge: 3 days
Freezer: up to 3 months
Freezing method: in a
    freezer bag, pancakes
    separated with baking paper

1. Add your flour, sweetcorn, cheese, spring onion and oregano to a bowl and mix until everything is coated in flour.

2. Add in your eggs and combine until you have a gloopy batter.

3. Heat the olive oil in a large frying pan over a medium-low heat.

4. Add heaped tablespoons of batter to the pan to make pancakes around 6cm in diameter. Cook for 2 minutes on each side until golden. You may need to do this in batches.

5. Cool on a wire rack.

6. Serve with my tomato dip (page 194).

What's good:

Minimal mess.

Delicious hot or cold: great to take for lunch out.

Spring onion: introduces a stronger flavour profile, has antibacterial and antiviral properties.

Pea & Ricotta Pinwheels

10 mins   20 mins   20 mins

VG   NF

Makes 12 pinwheels

75g frozen peas
60g ricotta cheese
1 sheet ready-made puff pastry
1 beaten egg (optional)
Sprinkle of grated cheese
   (optional)

Fridge: 3 days
Freezer: up to 2 months
Freezing method: freezer
   bag, separated with
   baking paper

Pinwheels are a weaning rite of passage. When Rue was about 4 months old, and I first dipped my toe into the world of 'wtf-is-weaning', I saw pinwheels absolutely everywhere! Pizza pinwheels are a great favourite in our house, but as I gave you a pizza recipe on page 104 I thought best not to overdo it, so let's try something fresh.

These pea and ricotta pinwheels are a great variation. Peas bring a subtle sweetness (and pack a good punch of iron and protein!), while creamy ricotta adds an indulgent edge. The combination of both wrapped in flaky puff pastry is *chef's kiss*... Can you still use that phrase when you are the chef? I just did.

1. Boil or steam your peas for 5 minutes until soft. Drain.

2. Add the ricotta cheese and the peas to a blender and whizz to a whipped purée.

3. Roll out your puff pastry flat and spread a thin layer of the pea and ricotta mixture all over the base, leaving a 1cm gap around the edge.

4. Gently but firmly roll up your puff pastry (like a Yule log!). You want the roll to be just tight enough to hold in the filling, but without squeezing out your pea mixture. Chill this for 20 minutes.

5. Cut your rolled-up tube into slices around 2.5cm thick, then lay these flat, spiral side up, on an oven tray lined with baking paper. Leave a bit of space between each. If you can't fit them all on one tray, put the spares into the fridge and bake them as another batch.

6. Brush each pinwheel with a thin layer of beaten egg, if you like, and sprinkle over some cheese, if desired. Cook according to your puff pastry instructions, usually around 12 minutes at 200°C (180°C fan).

7. Transfer the pinwheels to a wire rack and leave to cool before serving and storing.

What's good:

Ricotta: less salty than many cheeses and a good source of calcium.

Peas: plant-based protein and vitamin C.

Easy self-feeding and great for fussy feeders!

Tropical Yoghurt Bark

10 mins   2 hours

VG   GF   NF

Makes 4-6 large pieces of bark

100g full-fat Greek yoghurt
20g mango, blended to a purée
20g pineapple, finely chopped
Sprinkle of desiccated coconut

Freezer: up to 2 months

Yoghurt bark is the perfect way to experiment with cold temperatures; great for hot summer days and teething alike. The tropical flavours here are not just the result of my fondness for piña coladas – pineapple actually has anti-inflammatory properties, which make it a great addition for soothing teething gums.

Nutritionally the same as giving your baby yoghurt with fruit, the frozen aspect has the added bonus of being a brand-new sensory experience. Most babies get stuck right in, but don't be surprised if the initial reaction is shock or tears; extreme cold both in their hands and their mouths can be overwhelming! It doesn't take long for them to learn that it is, in fact, delicious. So much so that Rue will now cry when she realises it's all gone – I know the feeling, hun.

The topping choices here really are endless! Finely chopped blueberries or strawberries, grated apple or chopped banana all work well, too. For older toddlers and children you can add even more variety with sprinkles or even melted chocolate.

1. Use a freezer-friendly tub or tray and line it with baking paper. Leaving longer ends on the paper at each end of the tray will help you pull out the frozen yoghurt when the time comes.

2. Spread the Greek yoghurt across the base, keeping it as even as possible in depth.

3. Use sweeping motions, spread the mango purée through the yoghurt, then scatter the chopped pineapple and coconut evenly over the top. Place in the freezer for 2 hours.

4. Once your yoghurt has frozen, remove it from the freezer and let it stand until you can remove it from the tub.

5. Smash the slab of yoghurt bark to break it into portion-sized pieces. Pop the pieces into a freezer bag ready to grab whenever you want to give your baby a frozen treat!

What's good:

Yoghurt: rich in calcium and good bacteria.

Pineapple: enzymes that help protect against inflammation.

Frozen food: sensory development.

Cinnamon Teething Biscuits

15 mins   20 mins

VG   NF

Makes 12-15 biscuits

75g unsalted butter (at room
  temperature)
1 egg
1 tsp vanilla extract
100g quick-cook smooth
  porridge oats
15g ground golden flaxseed
30g plain flour, plus extra for
  dusting
2 tsp ground cinnamon
1 tsp baking powder

Flavourings (optional):
1 tbsp peanut butter
Mashed banana
Fruit purée

Fridge: 4 days
Freezer: 2 months
Freezing method: flash
  freeze and transfer
  to freezer bags

These teething biscuits are a lovely little all-rounder, with a healthy dose of iron and calcium from fortified oats, plenty of healthy fats, and anti-inflammatory benefits from cinnamon. They make the perfect substitute for store-bought snacks, which are often packed full of sneaky sugars and preservatives.

1. Preheat the oven to 190°C (170°C fan).

2. In a large mixing bowl, use a hand-held electric mixer to beat the butter until smooth, then add in your egg and vanilla extract and combine.

3. In a separate bowl, mix together the oats, flaxseed, flour, cinnamon and baking powder.

4. Gradually add your dry ingredients to the butter and egg mixture, folding them in well, then add in any other flavourings. Combine with a spoon and then your hand to bring the dough together.

5. On a lightly floured surface, roll out your dough to around 1cm thickness, then use a cookie cutter or a glass to cut out your biscuits. Alternatively, you could cut them into rectangles like traditional cereal bars.

6. Pop them on a tray lined with baking paper and cook for 15–20 minutes until just starting to turn golden.

7. Transfer to a wire rack and leave to cool before serving and storing.

What's good:

Less sugar than shop-bought: better for emerging teeth.

Cinnamon: anti-inflammatory to help soothe sore gums.

Gaining Confidence (10–11 months)

Breakfasts

Lunches

Dinners

On the Go

Celebration!

Breakfasts

Lunches

Dinners

On the Go

Celebration!

STAGE

3

Stage 3: Gaining Confidence (10–11 months)

One thing about babies is they're always going to surprise you with the massive leaps in development and skills that they can make in a relatively short time. This is a really fun period of weaning; there's much less gagging and much more interest in what they're eating. You might notice them turning things over in their hands, enjoying taking foods apart, inspecting the fillings of a wrap closely or picking particular veggies out of a curry.

Just to give you an idea of how quickly skills can develop and change, in every single meal when Rue was 10 months, the first thing she would do was find her cutlery and toss it off the side of her highchair. Watching it back in my meal videos is quite entertaining, as she did this with the air of someone swatting away a fly, or like royalty dismissing a disgraced subject. I could almost hear her saying, 'Why does this woman insist on cluttering up my plate with this useless article?'. But by the time she reached 11.5 months, a matter of a few weeks later, she was opting to pick up her preloaded cutlery and eat from it without any encouragement from me. I was so glad that I'd stuck with offering cutlery at every meal (there were many occasions where I thought, 'What's the point?'), and it just goes to show that you never know when a skill is going to fall into place!

Skills

- Eating food with greater dexterity, using a range of grips.

- Continue to offer and preload cutlery for some mouthfuls, they may start to show more interest in dipping/scooping and their cutlery in general (don't worry if they don't, but you can also try tip number 2 below if you do want to get the ball rolling with it).

What to expect

▶ Continue to adjust/reduce milk feeds in line with more efficient eating. This can still be a flexible process, if you think your baby has not eaten much during their solids meals you can up their milk, and similarly if they have a good day of eating, you might offer less milk.

▶ Food stuffing might become more common at this stage. Try to remember it is a normal developmental phase (I explain why in more detail in the Troubleshooting section on page 48). Avoid putting your fingers in their mouth to get food out and give them time to work out their own next steps.

Top tips

★ Experiment with some bigger flavours, such as subtle heat. Aim to keep things mild and gently increase the intensity from there. You don't want to scare them, put them off or cause any tummy pain or fiery toilet experiences!

★ Model dipping and scooping with exaggeration when preloading their cutlery. Use consistent phrases such as 'scoop scoop' or 'in and up' to draw your baby's attention to what you are doing (and hopefully get them thinking about trying it themselves one day!).

★ P.S. With the big birthday on the horizon, be sure to check out my no-added-sugar first Birthday Cake recipe on page 140.

Banana Pancakes

10 mins   15 mins

VG   NF

Makes 8 10cm adult pancakes and 10 5cm baby pancakes, or 24 5cm baby pancakes

2 small, overripe bananas
2 eggs
190ml milk
20ml vegetable oil or 20g
   unsalted butter, melted
240g plain flour
1 tsp baking powder

Greek yoghurt and berries,
   to serve

Fridge: 4 days
Freezer: up to 3 months
Freezing method: freezer
   bag, separated with
   baking paper

These pancakes are a sacred Sunday tradition for us. The delight of thick, fluffy pancakes, the sweetness of banana and, best of all, no added sugar makes these so perfect for all ages. Overripe bananas work best here and will achieve the fluffiest pancakes, but I've made them with just-ripe bananas before and still had great results. Make a stack for the adults and use up the rest making baby-sized pancakes for the freezer stash!

1. In a large mixing bowl, mash your bananas and add in your eggs, milk and vegetable oil or butter.

2. In a separate bowl, sift together your flour and baking powder.

3. Slowly fold your dry ingredients into the wet, stirring continually. Leave to rest as you heat a non-stick pan over a medium heat.

4. Drop 1 generous tablespoon per baby pancake into the hot pan and 3 generous tablespoons for adult pancakes (roughly 10cm in diameter). Wait until a few bubbles appear on the surface of the batter before flipping, this should take around 2–3 minutes. If your first pancakes don't look golden enough in this time, turn the heat up slightly. Cook for a further 2 minutes on the second side.

5. Transfer to plates and pop any extras on a wire rack to cool before storing/serving.

6. Serve with Greek yoghurt, strawberries and/or blueberries (squished for babies).

What's good:

Easy self-feeding.

Perfect grab-and-go for breakfasts out.

Banana: potassium and natural sweetness.

Fussy-feeder-friendly.

Egg Cups

15 mins   28 mins

VG   GF   NF

Makes 10 egg cups

Unsalted butter, for greasing
5 eggs
100g full-fat cottage cheese
40g finely sliced red pepper
   or tomato (or both!)
Sprinkle of grated cheese to
   top (optional)

*I have previously
experimented with whisking
and/or blending this recipe
and the resulting egg cups
are not as nice in texture.
Mixing with a fork seems to
be the best way!

Fridge: 3 days
Freezer: up to 3 months
Freezing method: wrap in
   cling film and pop into a
   freezer bag. Defrost in the
   fridge overnight or using
   your microwave's defrost
   settings

It took me a long while to settle on an egg cup recipe I was happy with. As previously mentioned, I am a fussy gus when it comes to eggs and can't bring myself to subject Rue to anything I wouldn't eat. I've experimented with many variations of egg cups throughout weaning and they've ranged from too spongy or too bland, to drier than the Sahara desert.

My mission was to create an egg cup that wasn't dry, was packed with flavour and was still nice when reheated for future meals. I can safely say this recipe ticks all of those boxes, and it's actually very simple which is obviously a bonus! The addition of cottage cheese gives the egg cups added creaminess, and cooking them low and slow means they retain their moisture really well. The addition of red pepper or tomatoes gives the boost of vitamin C needed to help with iron absorption from the eggs.

1. Preheat the oven to 140°C (120°C fan). Grease a muffin tray with some unsalted butter, or use silicone muffin cases (I prefer to do this for easy removal).

2. Crack the eggs into a mixing jug, add the cottage cheese and combine with a fork. At first, it will seem like the egg and cottage cheese do not want to mix, but keep going and eventually they will fold into one another.* The mixture will still be lumpy due to the cottage cheese, but that's fine.

3. Pour your mixture into the muffin cases, filling them to just above halfway, then add a few chunks of finely sliced veggies to each egg cup and finish with a sprinkle of grated cheese, if using.

4. Place on the middle shelf of the oven for 28 minutes. Pop a skewer in and check it comes out clean, to ensure the egg is cooked all the way through.

5. Serve 2 or 3 egg cups on their own, with a dipping sauce (see page 194) or with a side of buttered toast. Leave the rest to cool on a wire rack before storing.

What's good:

Packed with protein: from the eggs and cottage cheese.

Cottage cheese: a great source of calcium and B vitamins.

Red pepper: rich in vitamin C.

Fruity French Toast

5 mins   10 mins

VG   NF

Makes 1 adult portion and 1 baby portion, or 2–3 baby portions

1 small, ripe banana
A handful of blueberries (or 2 strawberries)
1 egg
20ml milk
Knob of unsalted butter
3–4 small slices of wholemeal bread

Plain yoghurt and some fresh berries, to serve

Fridge: in an airtight container for 2 days

It took me a while to master French toast for baby-led weaning. To my mind, French toast is super indulgent: thick, fried, doughy brioche bread, lathered in berries, whipped cream, maple syrup and/or icing sugar. In the words of Miss Trunchbull, 'far too good for children'.

Obviously, for babies the aim is to scale back the sweetness significantly from the versions that I might order at brunch. I had many failed French toast experiments that came out more like eggy bread, and although Rue ate them all, the flavour and fun of the dish just wasn't there. This version hits the mark for us; the sweetness of the fruit soaks into the bread and disguises the egg. If you're not a fan of banana, simply leave it out and up the berries!

1. Blend your banana, blueberries (or strawberries), egg and milk together and pour the mixture into a wide, flat bowl.

2. Heat a pan over a medium-high heat and melt the butter.

3. Lay a slice of bread in the fruit batter, leave it to soak for 30 seconds, then flip to repeat on the other side.

4. Transfer the slice of bread to the pan. Cook for around 3 minutes on each side, until the egg is cooked and the bread is golden. Repeat the soaking and frying process until the mixture has been used up!

5. Serve with a dollop of plain yoghurt and some fresh berries.

What's good:

A twist on traditional toast: maintains a wide variety of textures and presentations of foods.

Eggs: healthy fats and nutrient-rich.

Wholemeal bread: a filling and fibrous breakfast.

Pasta – Eight Ways

Pasta is comfort food. It's great for weaning because babies tend to love it, and with the right sauce it can be a vehicle for many hidden veggies. Be aware that pasta can be a culprit for gagging, but it is not a common choking hazard, so allow your little one to work through those moments and figure out how much they need to chew it. Bigger shapes like fussiloni are great for smaller babies as they are easier to hold, but the options really are endless. We love Spaghetti Bolognese (page 106) and my Lentil Pasta Sauce (page 64), but there are plenty of times when I'm in need of something speedier. Here are eight of my favourite go-tos for an easy and quick pasta dish:

1. Sardines and Passata (DF NF)

Another super-simple two-ingredient option. Sardines are a great oily fish option for little ones and they're also very affordable in comparison to other fish choices. Add a tin of sardines to a blender with 250–500g of passata (depending on how much sauce you'd like to end up with) and blend it all together. Similar to tinned salmon, the bones in tinned sardines are soft and will blend down easily. They also add a boost of calcium to the sauce!

2. Salmon and Mayonnaise (NF)

Similar to tuna pasta, but more friendly to little ones as this option is lower in mercury. Use tinned or freshly cooked salmon fillet, flake the pieces and mix well with mayonnaise and cooked pasta.

3. Avocado and Tomato (V VG DF NF)

All that's needed for this sauce is some mashed avocado (however much you need for your pasta portion), quartered cherry tomatoes and a little dash of olive oil. Coat the pasta well and eat it fresh!

4. Broccoli and Cream Cheese (VG NF)

A super-easy, two-ingredient sauce. Simply steam and mash or finely chop some broccoli, add it to a bowl of cooked pasta with a few tablespoons of full-fat cream cheese and mix it all well. Add a sprinkle of hemp seeds for a boost of protein. For adult portions, add some chilli flakes for a kick.

5. Pesto (VG)

Pop 30g pine nuts into a blender or food processor and pulse them to a fine consistency. Add 50g basil and 20g freshly grated Parmesan (and some chopped garlic, if desired) and pulse again. Add 50ml olive oil and blend everything together to a creamy consistency. For a looser texture, continue to add olive oil or water in ½ tablespoon measures until it's the texture you like.

6. Butternut Squash and Garlic (V VG DF NF)

Preheat the oven to 180°C (160°C fan). Cut a butternut squash in half and remove the seeds. In a large roasting dish, place your squash, a whole bulb of garlic and 3 or 4 tomatoes. Add a drizzle of olive oil, a sprinkle of smoked paprika, then roast for 40 minutes. Once roasted, add all the contents to a blender – scoop the squash out of the skin, squeeze the garlic bulb to release the softly cooked garlic and add in your tomatoes (without the skin, where possible). Blend it all together, then toss with freshly cooked pasta. The remaining sauce can be left to cool and then stored in the fridge for 3 days or freezer for 3 months (freeze in portions).

7. Houmous (V VG DF NF)

Use the houmous recipe from page 66 and mix into cooked pasta. Top with a sprinkle of hemp seeds for added grip!

8. Red Pepper (V VG DF NF)

Roast 2 or 3 red peppers for 20 minutes at 200°C (180°C fan), or until you see them soften and the skin is darkened/collapsed. Once roasted, remove the skin and add the peppers to a blender with a tin of chopped tomatoes and a teaspoon of garlic powder. Whizz into a sauce and stir into freshly cooked pasta. Extra portions can be stored in the fridge for up to 3 days or the freezer for up to 3 months.

Savoury Scones

15 mins   10 mins

VG   NF

Makes 10–12 scones

300g self-raising flour, plus
    extra for dusting
1 tsp baking powder
80g ground flaxseed
80g unsalted butter, cut into
    cubes
180ml milk
Splash of lemon juice
1 beaten egg

Flavourings (optional):
1 spring onion, finely chopped
½ carrot, grated
30g cheese, grated

Fridge: 4 days
Freezer: up to 3 months
    (before or after cooking)
Freezing method: if cooked,
    in a freezer bag; if
    uncooked, portion into
    individual scone sizes,
    wrap in cling film and pop
    in a freezer bag

This recipe is one of my favourites to make. Traditional and super easy, there is nothing more satisfying than enjoying a warm scone straight from the oven.

This savoury spring onion twist makes it a great lunch option, but there are so many different things you can add to this mixture. I use flaxseed to give them a nutrient super boost (I use ground golden flaxseed but brown is fine too). It also adds a lovely rustic element to the dough and the resulting scones are delicious... if I do say so myself! You could even halve the dough and make some sweeter varieties too: apple and cinnamon, pear, raisins* or blueberries all work beautifully. Or simply leave them plain and add a layer of unsalted butter or chia jam. The opportunities are endless! Can you tell I'm excited about scones?

*Raisins are high in sugar so use them sparingly. For smaller babies, grated apple, pear or blueberries would be a better option.

1. Preheat the oven to 220°C (200°C fan).

2. Add the flour, baking powder and flaxseed to a large mixing bowl. Use your hands to rub the butter into the flour until you're left with a mixture that resembles fine breadcrumbs. (This is the longest part of the process. It's an endurance task. It takes about 5 minutes and during that time your hands will cramp and you might want to give up. Keep going. No pain, no gain, as they say.)

3. Warm your milk for 30 seconds in the microwave and then add in your lemon juice.

4. Combine your liquids into your mixing bowl. I fold it all together with a cutlery knife – don't ask me why, it's just the best tool for the job. If you're making any plain scones, or ones with different flavours, divide your dough now – add your spring onion, carrot and around half of your cheese.

5. Put your dough onto a lightly floured surface. Don't over-knead it because your scones might end up tough. Flatten to about 3cm thickness and cut out your shapes. You can use the top of a glass for traditional round scones, or form them into finger shapes for snack-sized baby scones. Fold, flatten and cut out the leftover dough until you've used it all.

6. Brush the top of your scones with beaten egg, sprinkle the remaining cheese on top and pop them on your baking tray. Arrange the scones close together to encourage them to rise upwards instead of outwards. Bake for 10 minutes until risen and golden on top.

7. Transfer to a wire rack and leave to cool before serving or storing.

What's good:

Flaxseed: omega 3s for brain development, fibre for a healthy gut microbiome.

Scones: a less-mess meal and great for fussy feeders.

Veggie Chilli

10 mins   35 mins

NF	DF	GF	V	VG

Makes 8–10 baby portions, or 2 adult portions and 4 baby portions

1 onion, diced
Olive oil, for cooking
1 tbsp tomato purée
1 tsp ground cumin*
1 carrot, peeled and diced
1 small sweet potato, peeled and diced**
1 x 400g tin of chopped tomatoes
300ml baby-friendly stock (any preferred flavour: beef, chicken or vegetable)
1 x 198g tin of kidney beans (approx. 130g drained weight), rinsed
1 x 198g tin of cannellini or butter beans, rinsed
1 x 198g tin of sweetcorn (reduced salt), rinsed

Tortilla wrap or flatbread (or gluten-free alternative), to serve

Fridge: 4 days
Freezer: up to 3 months
Freezing method: allow to cool, then portion into freezer bags

This Veggie Chilli is one of the easiest whole-family meals ever. It's my go-to for batch cooking because it requires barely any memory or skill to throw together (music to my ears) and many of the ingredients are tinned items that can sit ready and waiting in the cupboard. Once you've made it, you will see how easy it is to chuck everything into the pan and leave it to do its thing.

It's not just a favourite from a cooking perspective. This is hands down one of Rue's favourite dinners. Even now that we've entered a more selective phase of eating, she will still get stuck into this meal without a second thought. A winner all round!

1. Heat a pan over a medium heat and add the onion with some olive oil.

2. In a small bowl, mix your tomato purée with the cumin and add to the pan. Stir everything together and allow it to heat through.

3. Add the carrot and sweet potato to the pan and stir, followed by the tin of chopped tomatoes and stock. Ensure the carrot and sweet potato chunks are submerged in liquid – add more water if there doesn't seem enough. Leave this to heat through and come to the boil.

4. Add the kidney beans, cannellini beans and sweetcorn to your chilli pot. Gently push them down into the liquid. Cover and cook for 20 minutes, then uncover, stir and leave for a further 10 minutes or until reduced to your desired consistency.

5. Once your chilli is done, the carrot, sweet potato and beans should all be soft and mushy in texture. When serving, you can gently flatten or mash any pieces you aren't comfortable with.

6. Serve with some fingers of toasted flatbread. This chilli also works nicely as the filling in a quesadilla for a less messy lunch option!

*You can also add cayenne pepper if you want to introduce some heat to the dish.
**For the sweet potato, cut them into rounds of about 1cm thickness, then cut each round into quarters. For the carrot, cut into 1cm round slices, then halve each slice.

What's good:
Kidney beans: support healthy blood, development and growth

Rich in plant-based protein sources

Great for the whole family

Mango Chicken Curry

10 mins   45 mins

GF   NF

Makes 2 adult portions and 2 baby portions, or 6–8 baby portions

1 tbsp tomato purée
2 tsp garam masala
1 tsp smoked paprika
1 tsp onion granules
1 tsp garlic paste or powder
Sprinkle of dried coriander leaf
300–500g skinless, boneless
    chicken breast, cut into
    thin strips
Olive oil, for frying
4 tomatoes, chopped
1 small mango, peeled and
    chopped (or use frozen
    chunks)
1 x 400ml tin of coconut milk
Rice or a homemade
    flatbread (page 156, or GF
    alternative).

Fridge: 2 days
Freezer: up to 3 months
Freezing method: portion
    into freezer bags

Who doesn't love a curry? I'm not ashamed to say that – second only to my child – this curry is my greatest achievement in life. It's so simple, so tasty and easily one of my most popular recipes. Creamy coconut milk and juicy mango pair with the acidity of tomato and the flavour of the spices to create something wonderful.

I will end my love letter here, but I hope you enjoy it just as much as we do!

1. Add your tomato purée, all of your spices and coriander leaf to a small bowl and mix into a paste.

2. In a large bowl, coat the chicken strips with the spice paste.

3. Gently heat the olive oil in a large pan, then add the chicken, and cook, turning occasionally until just starting to brown. Add the tomatoes, mango and coconut milk to the pan and bring it to the boil. Leave the pan uncovered and gently bubbling for 30–40 minutes, stirring occasionally, until the sauce has reduced.

4. Serve with rice or a homemade flatbread (page 156).

What's good:

Coconut and mango: a subtle sweetness that babies love!

Garam masala: aids digestion and good for heart health.

Curry: great for introducing a wider flavour and texture profile.

Meatballs

20 mins   20 mins

GF   NF

Makes around 8 meatballs

1 egg*
½ tbsp tomato purée
250g beef mince
½ carrot, grated
½ onion, grated
1 tsp dried thyme, oregano
    or basil
1 tsp garlic granules
A sprinkle of black pepper
20g grated cheese

*Egg works to bind this dish together, but if you can't use egg it is still possible to form the meatballs without it. You could also consider using applesauce or a flax egg as a replacement.

Fridge: 3 days
Freezer: up to 2 months
Freezing method: can
    be frozen uncooked or
    cooked; flash freeze, then
    transfer to a freezer bag

Meatballs are a great companion to baby-led weaning. You're simply taking a mince-based meal, compacting it and presenting it in a simple, easy-to-feed way! This recipe could use any mince: lamb, pork, turkey or even quorn if you are veggie. Beef, however, is an amazing source of nutrients and the haem iron found in meats is more easily absorbed by the body – nearly six times better than non-haem iron found in plants. For this reason alone it's a great food to incorporate in your baby's diet from time to time.

When shaping your meatballs, go big or go home. You want to avoid small meatballs that could easily be put into the mouth whole. Aim for 4–5cm in diameter. If your little one does manage to stuff a whole meatball in, don't panic. They will soon discover that they cannot easily or comfortably eat it this way and will spit some, or all of it, back out.

1. Preheat the oven to 200°C (180°C fan).

2. Crack your egg into a small bowl, mix in the tomato purée and set to one side.

3. In a large bowl, mix together all of your other ingredients – mince, veggies and seasonings. The easiest way to do this is with your hands!

4. Add your egg mixture and combine, then start to shape your meatballs. Aim for a large size (around the size of a golf ball).

5. Pop them in the oven for 20 minutes, or cook in the pan or air fryer (180°C) for 15–18 minutes. The centre of a cooked meatball should read 70°C on a meat thermometer, or be visibly cooked through once cut open.

6. Serve 2 meatballs, whole or halved, alongside some pasta (or gluten-free alternative) in Lentil Pasta Sauce (page 64).

What's good: Beef: rich in essential nutrients including B vitamins and easy-to-absorb haem iron.

Meatballs make easy self-feeding.

Broccoli Twists

20 mins   15 mins

VG   NF

Makes 12 twists

1 sheet of ready-made puff
    pastry
1 beaten egg (optional)
40–50g broccoli, steamed and
    mashed
20g grated cheese
3 cherry tomatoes, thinly
    chopped
Sprinkle of dried oregano

Yoghurt topped with chia
    seeds, to serve

Fridge: 4 days
Freezer: 3 months
Freezing method: freezer
    bag separated with baking
    paper

There's just something about broccoli. It's a top tier vegetable. It's also full of goodness and incredibly versatile. These twists offer a nice variation on the usual tomato bases you find on puff pastry and they are also a perfect grab-and-go option as they freeze, reheat and travel really well!

My one top tip for this recipe would be to start working with your puff pastry as soon as it comes out of the fridge, and to work as quickly as you can. If you take too long, your pastry will be warm, sticky and difficult to shape, and that's not a combination anybody wants in life. Don't worry about the twists looking too perfect, puff pastry is very forgiving in that once it's cooked it all looks delicious either way!

1. Preheat the oven to 200°C (180°C fan).

2. Unroll your puff pastry and cut it in half lengthways. Brush both halves with the beaten egg, if using.

3. Using just the bottom half of the pastry, spread your mashed broccoli in a thin layer, leaving a small gap at the edges of the pastry. Spread the grated cheese and chopped tomato evenly across the broccoli and top with a sprinkle of oregano.

4. Fold the top half of the pastry over the bottom half, beaten egg side down. You should now essentially have a sandwich of pastry, broccoli filling, pastry. Lightly roll a rolling pin over the top to compress it and then cut into uniform slices (around 4cm thick).

5. To create a twist, pick up a slice and gently fold it over, once in the middle and then again at either end. Try not to squeeze out any filling in the process.

6. Place the twists on to a tray lined with baking paper, brush with the remaining beaten egg, if using, then cook them according to the instructions on your puff pastry – usually around 12 minutes.

7. Leave to cool on a wire rack. Serve with yoghurt topped with chia seeds.

What's good:

Broccoli: a good source of plant-based iron and vitamin C.

Pastry twists: easy self-feeding.

A great option for on-the-go lunches.

Birthday Cake

20 mins   25 mins

VG   NF

For a 5-tier, 10cm cake

50g unsalted butter
3 medium, overripe bananas
2 eggs
120ml buttermilk
200g plain flour
1 tsp vanilla extract
1 tsp baking powder
½ tsp bicarbonate of soda
¼ tsp salt*

*Optional depending on baby's age

For the frosting and decoration:**
1 Medjool date, stoned
200ml whipping cream
Sprinkles, fruit slices or berries, to decorate

**You can also make frosting using cream cheese and fruit purée, or even avocado with cocoa powder!

Fridge: 1 day (frosted)
Freezer: freezing birthday cake is a crime, but the sponges could be frozen if needed. I wouldn't advise doing things too far in advance for this particular recipe, you want everything at its freshest and best!

Your baby's first birthday. There's something so official about one. It's a milestone for them and us both. And while it's a huge celebration, we know as parents that it is tinged with a happy kind of sorrow. We've been given a handful of years to cherish with them, and this is the first one spent.

Sobbing aside, take some time to reflect on how far you have come as a parent. The obstacles and learning curves you've navigated. To top it all off, you are officially 6 months into weaning and should feel a great sense of achievement about that alone!

This Birthday Cake recipe is no-added sugar, perfect for a cake smash or to be shared and enjoyed on the big day. Although it has many tiers, it is a baby-sized cake, so if you're hoping to feed a large party I would recommend increasing all quantities to suit your needs.

1. Preheat the oven to 200°C (180°C fan).

2. In a large mixing bowl, add your butter and mix to soften.

3. Mash the bananas (or blend for an ultra-smooth consistency), then add the banana, eggs and buttermilk to the butter and combine. Fold in your flour, vanilla, baking powder, bicarbonate of soda and salt.

4. Divide the batter equally among five 10-cm silicone cake moulds.

5. Place on the middle shelf of your oven. Cook for 20–25 minutes, until a skewer inserted into the middle of a cake comes out clean. Allow to fully cool on a wire rack.

6. For the frosting, soak the date in a splash of boiling water in a small bowl and leave for 5–10 minutes.

7. Add your whipping cream and use an electric whisk or hand blender to whip to a thick consistency.

8. Cut the baked tops and bottoms from your sponges (these aren't part of the final cake but you can still enjoy them with a cup of tea!). Build your cake tiers. Sponge on the bottom, a layer of frosting, sponge, a layer of frosting and repeat.

9. Once your tiers are built, spread the remainder of the frosting evenly across the whole exterior of the cake. This doesn't need to be neat, naked cakes are all the rage!

10. You can decorate your cake further, if desired, with sprinkles, fruit slices or berries.

11. Due to the whipped cream frosting, store your cake in the fridge until serving. It's best to frost it on the day if possible, but it can also be left overnight. I wouldn't advise doing it any more than 24 hours in advance.

What's good:

No added sugar.

Deliciousness.

Cake!

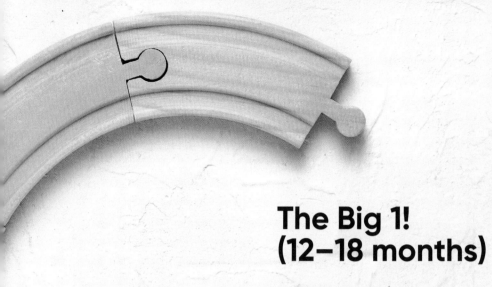

The Big 1!
(12–18 months)

Breakfasts

Lunches

Dinners

Snacks

Breakfasts

Lunches

Dinners

Snacks

STAGE

4

Stage 4:
The Big 1!
(12–18 months)

Are you feeling emosh?! Your baby turning one is a momentous occasion. From this point on in weaning there are a few minor changes, but continuing to offer wholesome and nutritious meals will mean you are ticking off the boxes easily. From 12 months, babies need a little more protein and a little less iron (but iron-rich foods are still important and you should continue to prioritise them). You can relax the reins a tiny bit on their salt intake as they can now have up to 2g a day, but continue to be mindful of the amount you use. Honey is no longer considered dangerous, although it is full of sugar so it is not something to offer often. You can also make the transition to cow's milk instead of formula, which is great for your bank balance. Although, if your child is anything like mine, you are now spending a significant amount of money on blueberries, so you might not feel like you're saving much!

The other key change from 12 months is the introduction of snacks. I have some great ideas for snacks on page 164, but the most important things to remember are:

1. Try to maintain variety in textures and colours when offering snacks, as beige snacks can result in more fussiness at mealtimes.

2. Realistically, snacks might be eaten in a less formal environment as opposed to in their highchair, but it's important that they are still always supervised and safe (for example, sitting down rather than while on the move).

Skills

- Cutlery – Your little one may be ready to independently scoop. Some toddlers will let you guide their hand gently to do this, some don't like that approach and would rather work it out themselves! Soft foods and breakfast cereals are great practice for this.

- You may notice an increased interest in spoken language during this phase (perhaps you'll even have the joy of hearing your baby's first words!). Keep up conversations during meal times – they will really enjoy hearing the names of the foods they are eating.

What to expect

▶ 'Fussy' or selective eating might begin to creep in from this age. It's a normal developmental phase and you should try to continue to offer foods as before. Try not to substitute foods or offer alternatives, as this will narrow the types of food they are likely to accept in future.

Top tips for fussy eating

⭐ End the meal and try again with the same plate 30 minutes later – let hunger be the driver!

⭐ Maintain a clear, structured mealtime routine. Nobody likes being unprepared for something or interrupted from what they're doing unexpectedly. Let your toddler know a meal is coming up, 'You can play with your cars and then it will be time for dinner', then give 5 minutes' notice of a meal or snack. Try to keep clear steps in the routine, such as wash our hands, sit at the table, put on our bib, etc. These markers can really help keep mealtimes running smoothly.

⭐ Share a plate! Toddlers love eating your food, so let them believe they are. This wouldn't be something you do every mealtime, but it can be especially useful if you're introducing a new food, or something they haven't had in a while.

⭐ Play 'Cheers!' with food items. Say, 'Shall we both eat some carrot? Cheers!', then tap your food together and pop it into your mouth, and hopefully they will do the same. It's playful and it can get the ball rolling, as it's often the first bites of a meal that are the challenge.

⭐ Play some music in the background. Classical or gentle music works well, nothing too overstimulating. This can give them something else to focus on and massively reduces the pressure of mealtimes.

⭐ Let them help you prepare food. Do this safely, either on a table at their level or using a kitchen helper/learning tower. They can watch you and/or help, while you talk about the different foods you're using in the meal. They could:

- Transfer veggie peelings into a container or bowl.

- Pass you foods from the fridge or cupboard.

- Mix things, for example, in baking, or stirring fruit into yoghurt.

- Put bread in the toaster (switch the toaster off at the wall and ensure it's not hot).

- Help spread toppings on bread or toast.

- Pour things, such as milk onto cereal.

- Help grate foods, such as carrot.

- Peel the shells off hard-boiled eggs (once cooled enough).

- Put food items onto their own plate for a meal (once cooled enough).

- Help you to cut soft-cooked foods or fruits. Make sure you are doing this hand over hand, safely, with no fingers near blades. Use a child-friendly tool such as a children's knife or crinkle cutter. If cutting something rounded, like cucumber, prepare it first by cutting it in half lengthways, then place the flat edge on the surface so that it doesn't roll around as your little one is cutting it.

As time goes on and they get used to being in the kitchen there will be more and more tasks that they can help you with. It doesn't just get them engaged with mealtimes, it also expands their vocabulary, builds their understanding of how foods look before and after cooking and gives them great foundations for their own cookery skills.

Overnight Chia Oats

10 mins   2+ hours

VG   NF

Makes 1 serving

25g porridge oats
1 tsp chia seeds
65g milk of choice
1 large strawberry, finely
    chopped or mashed
1 tsp peanut butter (optional)
1 tbsp full-fat Greek or plain
    yoghurt
A few blueberries, chopped

Fridge: 3 days
Freezer: Once fully soaked
    (after at least 2 hours), you
    can freeze the mixture for
    up to 3 months

Overnight oats make a fun and convenient alternative to porridge – all the same key ingredients but with a creamier, richer consistency. The addition of chia seeds not only gives a boost of nutrients but also adds an edge to the overall texture. You can do your morning self a favour by making up a few servings at once, then all you need to do is grab it from the fridge at breakfast time.

This has an easy-to-scoop texture that sticks to the spoon well, making it great for some spoon practice for your little one. But don't worry if they reject cutlery altogether, I can't say I'd blame them for wanting to jump in with their hands for some sensory exploration. Bibs at the ready!

1. In a small container or bowl, mix your porridge oats and chia seeds together.

2. Pour over your milk and mix in your strawberry and peanut butter, if using. Stir well, making sure to scoop all the corners and edges of your container to move the liquid through the dry ingredients.

3. Pop the mixture into the fridge for 30 minutes (if you don't have time for this step, just make sure your mixture so far is very well stirred before continuing).

4. Remove from the fridge and give it another thorough stir. Giving chia seeds a chance to begin 'blooming' and then stirring them again reduces the chance of the seeds clumping. Clumped chia seeds are a choking hazard, so be thorough with your stirring.

5. Add the Greek yoghurt on top, and sprinkle over your chopped blueberries. Cover and refrigerate overnight, or for at least 2 hours.

What's good:

A nutritious grab-and-go breakfast and you can make a few portions at a time.

Soaked oats and chia seeds: a fun new texture to experience.

Chia seeds: omega 3s for brain development and high in calcium.

Cinnamon Banana Bites

10 mins   10 mins

Makes 2 baby servings

1 large banana
40g plain flour
50ml milk
½ tsp baking powder
½ tsp ground cinnamon
Oil, for cooking

Full-fat yoghurt and fresh
    berries, to serve

Fridge: 3 days
Freezer: these are best eaten
    fresh, but once cooled
    they could be frozen for
    up to 2 months. Defrost
    overnight in the fridge

Sweet, slightly caramelised banana with a pancakey outer coating...
need I say more? These bites are a perfect weekend breakfast when
you want something a little more indulgent but don't want to spend
too much time in the kitchen. They satisfy all the cravings, are quick
to make and are always a hit. Half a banana is more than enough for
a little one in one serving, especially with the pancake coating. You
can store the other half or eat them yourself (no two guesses what
happens in my house whenever I make them!).

1. Cut your banana in half lengthways, then split each half into its
   natural thirds (shown opposite).

2. In a wide, shallow bowl, whisk together your flour, milk, baking
   powder and cinnamon into a smooth batter. If it's too thick, add
   a little more milk to the batter.

3. Heat a pan over a medium heat with a small amount of oil.

4. Roll each piece of banana in the batter, aiming to coat each one
   equally, then fry them in the oil for 2–3 minutes on each side
   until golden.

5. Serve half a banana (3 thirds) with some full-fat yoghurt and
   fresh berries.

What's good:

The indulgence of pancakes in much less time.

Banana: great for energy and digestion.

Spinach and Apple Pancakes

Hulk pancakes! The colour may be so wrong, but the taste is so right. These pancakes have all the goodness of spinach but with the fresh, mild flavour of apples. This batter is made entirely in the blender, so it's nice and easy to whizz together, with minimal washing up. A great way to sneak in some veggies, I've served these pancakes as a breakfast or made them for snacks once Rue was older.

10 mins   15 mins

VG   NF

Makes 12 pancakes

100g spinach
1 small apple, peeled, cored
    and chopped
180ml milk
150g plain flour
2 tsp baking powder
1 egg
1 tbsp vegetable oil

Grated fresh apple or carrot,
    to serve

Fridge: 4 days
Freezer: up to 3 months
Freezing method: in a
    freezer bag, separated
    with baking paper

1. Heat a non-stick frying pan over a medium heat.

2. Place the spinach, apple and milk into the blender and blitz it until it's a smooth liquid.

3. Add in your flour, baking powder, egg and oil and blend it all together.

4. Pour your batter into the pan, aiming for pancakes around 6cm in diameter. This is a thin batter, so wait for 2–3 minutes until you can see the batter has started to darken in colour and numerous air bubbles have appeared, then flip your pancakes.

5. Serve 2–3 pancakes each topped with some grated fresh apple or carrot.

What's good:

Spinach: high in immunity-boosting antioxidants and supports brain health.

Apple: a good source of fibre and vitamin C.

Cauliflower Cheese Bites

15 mins   15 mins

VG   NF

Makes 16 bites

1 small cauliflower (approx.
    350g), stem removed
75g frozen peas
4 tbsp flaxseed
150g breadcrumbs (blend 2–3
    slices of bread in a blender)

For the cheese sauce:
25g unsalted butter
2 tbsp plain flour
250ml milk
25g Cheddar cheese, grated

Yoghurt dip and some fresh
    fruit, to serve (optional)

Fridge: 3 days
Freezer: up to 3 months
Freezing method: flash
    freeze, then transfer to
    freezer bag. Defrost in
    the oven or air-fry (150°C)
    from frozen for around
    15 minutes, turning at
    regular intervals, until
    heated through and crisp

It's a proven science that toddlers and children will eat almost anything if it resembles a nugget. These Cauliflower Cheese Bites are great; veggies in a creamy cheese sauce, all dressed up in a delicious crispy outer coating. They cook from frozen well, so are ideal to have in your freezer on standby for those days where you find yourself at a loose end for lunch or dinner. With the addition of flaxseed, these bites also contain a good amount of protein, so they are a complete meal for your little one.

1. Place the cauliflower in a microwaveable bowl with your peas, add a splash of water and microwave for 4 minutes.

2. Make the cheese sauce by melting the butter in a small saucepan over a medium heat. Once it's melted and frothy, gently add your flour while stirring continually to form a smooth paste. Gradually pour in your milk, stirring the whole time. Wait for the milk to heat up and start bubbling, then add in your grated cheese. Keep stirring until your cheese sauce thickens, then remove the pan from the heat.

3. Preheat your oven to 200°C (180°C fan).

4. In a large mixing bowl, mash your steamed cauliflower and peas with a fork. Add in your flaxseed and mix together.

5. Take your cheese sauce and add it to the cauliflower bit by bit, mixing at regular intervals. You want to add just enough that your mixture holds together. If you have cheese sauce left over, you can use this in pasta. It can even be frozen for up to 6 months for future use! Add around three-quarters of your breadcrumbs until your mixture forms a sticky dough.

6. Use your hands to form burger patty shapes, around 5cm in diameter and 2cm thick. Roll each in the remaining breadcrumbs to coat them.

7. Cook for 15 minutes, or until turning crispy on the outside, turning them over halfway through cooking.

8. Serve two on their own or with a yoghurt dip and some fresh fruit.

What's good:

Cauliflower: rich in vitamin C and vitamin K (essential for bone health).

Flaxseed: protein-rich and supports healthy brain development and digestion.

Quesadillas

10 mins   30 mins   20 mins

NF

Makes 4 quesadillas

½ chicken breast (around
    80g), roughly chopped
½ tsp smoked paprika
½ tsp garlic powder
½ tbsp olive oil, plus extra
    for frying
¼ red pepper, finely sliced
¼ yellow pepper, finely sliced
30g prune purée
4 mini tortilla wraps
80g cheese (mozzarella or
    Cheddar work well), grated

Dollop of sour cream, some
    thinly sliced cucumber
    and some quartered
    grapes, to serve

Fridge: 3 days
Freezer: up to 3 months
Freezing method: once
    cooled, wrap in cling film
    and freeze

I found this stage of weaning was a great time to introduce slightly more complicated textures, and quesadillas couldn't be more perfect. Toasted, slightly crisp tortilla wrap with oozy melty cheese and a variety of other fillings for your baby to explore and enjoy. They will benefit from eating this with you to see how it's done, but if they're still finding it a little overwhelming, you can always unfold the quesadilla and allow them to eat a deconstructed version. The filling options really are endless, but I love a simple chicken and peppers combination – with generous amounts of cheese, of course! Once cooked, the quesadillas can be stored in the fridge or freezer for future lunches.

1. Put the chicken in a bowl with the smoked paprika, garlic powder and olive oil. Mix well to coat the chicken, cover the bowl and pop it in the fridge for 15–30 minutes.

2. Heat a pan over a medium heat with a splash of olive oil. Add your seasoned chicken and cook until cooked through, then add the peppers and cook until softened.

3. Turn the heat to the lowest setting and add in the prune purée. Mix everything well to coat the chicken and peppers. Pop this mixture into a bowl and shred the chicken into small chunks.

4. Heat a clean pan over a medium heat.

5. Lay out your tortillas on a work surface and, using half of your cheese, add a layer to half of each tortilla (imagine each wrap is divided into semi-circles – sprinkle cheese on just the left half). On top of this, divide your chicken and pepper topping, sharing it equally between all the wraps, then finish with the remainder of your cheese and fold over each tortilla to enclose it all.

6. Add each quesadilla to your heated pan, cooking it for 2–3 minutes on each side until your tortilla turns golden and your cheese has melted.

7. To serve, cut in half (into pizza-slice shapes). Plate with a dollop of sour cream, some thinly sliced cucumber and some quartered grapes.

What's good:

Great for exploring hidden fillings.

Easy self-feeding.

A less-mess, portable lunch option.

Chunky Soup and Flatbread

20 mins   30 mins

VG   NF

Makes 2 adult portions and 2 baby portions

50g dried red lentils
1 carrot, peeled and chopped
   into ½cm dice
1 onion, chopped into ½cm
   dice
1 parsnip, peeled and
   chopped into ½cm dice
300ml baby-friendly
   vegetable stock

Per flatbread:
60g Greek yoghurt
50g self-raising flour, plus
   extra for dusting

Fridge: 3 days
Freezer: up to 3 months
Freezing method: portions
   in freezer bags

There's a reason soup is an established traditional dish in every culture around the world. Hearty, warming and versatile, it's the best way to use up any veggies, pulses or even meats that might otherwise go to waste. It freezes and reheats well, can be spicy or mild, can adapt with the seasons and comes in a variety of textures.

In terms of weaning and texture, it would be hard for a baby to self-feed creamy or brothy soups until they've got the hang of spoon scooping. For chunkier soups, such as this one, it's important to encourage your little one to chew (rather than slurp) so that they work through all the chunks of food hidden within. Luckily, that's simple enough to do with the addition of these flatbread soldiers. The fluffy, doughy flatbread not only provides a great vehicle for the soup, it also makes sure your little one is chewing throughout the meal. As always, eat with them, show them how and enjoy a tasty bowl together.

1. Put your lentils in a sieve and give them a thorough rinse. Add the lentils to a pan with the vegetables and your baby-friendly stock. Bring to the boil, stirring well, then reduce the heat, cover the pan and leave it to cook for 20–30 minutes.

2. While your soup cooks, in a mixing bowl combine your Greek yoghurt and flour. Bring it together until it forms a dough, but don't over-knead it otherwise your flatbreads will be tough when cooked.

3. Place the dough on a lightly floured surface and use a rolling pin to roll it into a flat circle, around ½cm thick.

4. Heat a pan to a medium heat. Wait for the pan to be hot before popping your flatbread in. Dry fry the flatbread (no oil) for 2–3 minutes on each side, until brown patches appear. Tear a small piece of the bread to check it is cooked through; if not, allow it a few more minutes on each side.

5. Once your soup is cooked and all the vegetables are soft, you can blend the soup to your desired consistency.

6. To serve, slice your flatbread into dipping soldiers and place these into the bowl for your baby to remove and eat. Adding the bread directly into the soup will also encourage your little one to chew, helping them navigate any chunks in the soup as well.

What's good:

Versatility!

Other veggies you could use: butternut squash, sweet potato, pumpkin, potato, pepper.

Other pulses you could use: kidney beans, cannellini beans, butter beans.

Spicy Lentil Nuggets

25 mins   25 mins

V   VG   NF   DF

Makes 10 nuggets

100g dried red lentils
50g carrot, grated
250ml water
1 tbsp medium curry powder
1 tsp garlic granules
1 tsp paprika
1 tsp ground cumin
Chilli paste/purée, to taste
50g breadcrumbs (1 slice, blended)
Olive oil, for drizzling

Fridge: 3 days
Freezer: up to 3 months
Freezing method: flash freeze, then transfer to a freezer bag

Spicy, you say? Absolutely, yes! There's no reason to shy away from introducing your baby to foods with a little more heat, and in fact many babies love it. For many cultures around the world, spicy foods are the norm. It will be a new sensation for your little one, so keep everything very mild at first. You want to allow them to experience it without being put off and without causing any irritation to their digestive system (which very hot foods can do). Of course, if you're uncomfortable with serving spice at this point, simply leave out the chilli paste. These nuggets are just as tasty and flavoursome without, so either way is fine.

1. Preheat the oven to 200°C (180°C fan).

2. Put your lentils in a sieve and give them a thorough rinse. Add the lentils to a large saucepan with the grated carrot and the water. Bring to the boil and allow to cook for 8–10 minutes until the water has mostly evaporated.

3. Add in your spices and mix well. Add your chilli paste bit by bit, until you can taste a very mild heat. Every chilli paste will vary, so start with ½ teaspoon and increase from there.

4. Cook off the remainder of the water, then take off the heat and transfer to a bowl, then add around three-quarters of your breadcrumbs and mix well. Leave until cool enough to handle.

5. Using a generous tablespoon of the mixture for each nugget, shape them by hand, then roll them in the remaining breadcrumbs.

6. Place the coated nuggets on a baking tray lined with baking paper, lightly drizzle on some oil for added crispiness. Cook for 20–25 minutes. All of the ingredients are technically cooked before they go in the oven, so this is just to crisp them up to your liking!

7. Serve these nuggets with a nice cooling dipping sauce (page 194) and eat alongside them to show them how it's done!

What's good:

Lentils: iron-rich and plant-based protein to support growth.

Spicy food: builds an adventurous palate.

Fish and Veggie Curry

10 mins   40 mins

GF   DF   NF

Makes 4 adult portions and 4 baby portions, or 12–15 baby portions

1½ tbsp curry powder
2 tbsp tomato purée
2 tbsp water
1 tbsp vegetable oil
1 garlic clove, crushed
1 onion, chopped
1 x 400ml tin of coconut milk
  (full-fat unsweetened)
3 frozen or fresh white fish
  fillets/steaks – pollock or
  cod (approx. 250g)
1 broccoli, chopped into
  small chunks
1 cauliflower, chopped into
  small chunks
1 x 400g tin of chopped
  tomatoes

Rice or flatbreads, to serve

Fridge: 3 days
Freezer: up to 3 months
Freezing method: freezer
  bags in portions

This curry is delicious and a great way to get fish into your little one's diet. Finned fish is an allergen, so for that reason alone keeping up exposures to it throughout weaning is a good idea. But on top of that, fish is a powerhouse of high-quality protein and supports heart health. Perfect for batch cooking, this recipe will take care of many dinners to come if you're just making it for your baby. I think it's a great one to cook for the whole family and enjoy together.

1. In a small bowl, combine the curry powder, tomato purée and water to create a spice paste.

2. Heat the vegetable oil in a pan over a medium heat. Add in the crushed garlic followed by your onion. Once the onion begins to soften, add in your spice paste and stir well to allow the flavours to heat through.

3. Add in the tin of coconut milk and stir well.

4. Take your fish fillets and place them into the liquid so they are submerged. Add your broccoli, cauliflower and tin of chopped tomatoes on top and stir gently. Once the contents are bubbling, cover your pan and leave for 5 minutes.

5. Uncover and stir well, breaking up your now-soft fish with the wooden spoon. Leave the curry uncovered for a further 20–30 minutes until it has reduced to your desired consistency.

6. Serve with rice or flatbreads, or a gluten-free alternative.

What's good:

Spices: introducing more complex flavours.

White fish: a good source of protein, iron and iodine for regulating metabolism.

Coconut milk: anti-inflammatory, anti-microbial and anti-fungal properties.

Turkey Burgers

15 mins   20 mins

VG   NF

Makes around 6 small burgers

1 x 400g tin of cannellini
    beans (around 200g drained)
50g butter
1 apple, peeled and diced
250g turkey mince
½ tsp onion powder

Full-fat yoghurt, fresh
    cucumber and diced
    potatoes, to serve

Fridge: 3 days
Freezer: up to 3 months
Freezing method: before or
    after cooking, flash freeze,
    then transfer to a freezer
    bag. Defrost in the fridge
    overnight

A meat and bean burger hybrid, these are perfect for self-feeding. They can also be made more complex as your little one gets older, as you can introduce the addition of a bun and other salad toppings! Cooking the apple in butter and puréeing it first not only adds that subtle hint of sweetness to the overall flavour, but also keeps these burgers juicy and far from dry.

Steps 4 and 5 in this recipe can be achieved much more quickly by using a food processor, if you have one. But if not, there's nothing wrong with some good old-fashioned chopping, mashing and mixing by hand!

1. Preheat the oven to 180°C (160°C fan).

2. Empty all the contents of your cannellini beans (including liquid) into a microwaveable bowl. Loosely cover and cook in the microwave on High for 1 minute 30 seconds. Drain and rinse the beans and transfer to a large mixing bowl.

3. In a pan over a medium-low heat, add your butter and apple pieces. Cover and leave for around 10 minutes for the apple to soften.

4. Use a hand blender or mash by hand to turn your apple to a purée.

5. Blend or mash by hand the beans until they are broken down, then add your turkey mince, onion powder and the apple purée to the bowl and combine it all well.

6. Shape your mixture into patties around 5cm in diameter, place the burger patties onto a tray lined with baking paper and cook for 20 minutes, turning halfway.

7. Serve with full-fat yoghurt as a dip, fresh cucumber and some diced potatoes.

What's good:

Turkey: contains all B vitamins, key to healthy immunity and development.

Cannellini beans: fibre rich and iron-rich.

Burgers: easy self-feeding.

Quick No-Cook Snacks

'Can I have a snack?'

Although you might not have heard this sentence directly from your child (yet), it's one that is warming up ready to be said over and over and over again when those verbal skills catch up! Snacks are the basis of a toddler's existence. When Rue was around 14 months, I remember thinking to myself, 'She just doesn't seem that bothered about snacks!' I was giving her three meals and one snack a day at this point, and I wasn't even sure if she really needed the extra. Then something happened. All of a sudden, she got the memo... and she got it big time!

The key thing to remember about snacks is that variety is still important. Around this age in particular, neophobia (fear of new things) starts to set in around foods and 'fussy' eating begins to rear its head. It's important to remember that snacks are part of the overall food strategy, so if we resort to offering the same very beige snacks day in day out, this is what children will become accustomed to. Although we as adults know a snack is a snack and a meal is a meal, to a toddler it is simply 'food I have been offered'. Including different colours, textures, flavours and veggies during snack time can really help to maintain a broader range of what your toddler will accept during other mealtimes, too.

But thankfully, that doesn't mean you have to be super organised in the kitchen. You just need a few tricks up your sleeve. Here are ten quick snack ideas that require no cooking whatsoever and can be made in under 5 minutes.

Mini crackers, cheese chunks and thin apple slices. (VG NF)

Mix 1 tablespoon of tahini with some ground cinnamon and serve with breadsticks to dip. (V VG DF NF)

Peanut butter and 'jelly' roll-ups. Take a slice of bread, cut off the crusts and roll it flat with a rolling pin. Spread over a very thin layer of peanut butter, then mash down some fresh raspberries on top. Roll up like a Swiss roll – et voilà! (V VG DF)

A crispbread topped with some mashed avocado. (V VG DF NF)

A plain rice cake spread with a thin layer of Greek yoghurt and topped with grated apple. (VG NF GF – check label)

Half a toasted wholemeal pitta with some store-bought salsa to dip. (V VG DF NF)

Half a crumpet spread with unsalted butter and served with some fruit. (VG NF)

Houmous, thinly sliced red pepper and a few mini breadsticks. (V VG NF DF)

Greek yoghurt with half a chopped banana. (VG GF NF)

A cream cracker spread with cream cheese. Top with a sprinkle of hemp seeds and some grated carrot. (VG NF)

Sweet Potato Bars

20 mins   12 mins

VG   NF

Makes 12–14 bars

250g steamed sweet potato
   (roughly 300–350g when raw)
1 small apple, grated
50g unsalted butter, melted
300g self-raising flour, plus
   extra for dusting
1 tsp ground cinnamon

Optional (both will add sugar):
1 tbsp honey (never give
   honey to under-1s)
20g dark chocolate, melted

Fridge: up to 4 days (I like
   to bring them out and
   allow them to come
   closer to room temp
   before eating)
Freezer: up to 2 months
Freezing method: flash
   freeze, then transfer
   to a freezer bag. Defrost
   in the fridge overnight,
   in the microwave or
   simply remove a bar
   from the freezer a few
   hours before eating

If you haven't realised by now, I am a big fan of sweet potatoes. Packed with nutrients like iron, vitamin C and beta carotene, they fight inflammation, enhance brain function and boost immunity. Their subtle sweetness makes them incredibly versatile – these bars are very straightforward to make and are rich in energy and fibre, so they are perfect for a filling snack.

Shop-bought snack bars, while convenient and great for certain situations, can contain unnecessary levels of free sugars and undesirable oils and preservatives. They're also quite costly, and often that's for a box of just five or six bars. I find having these homemade options the perfect solution – they're nutritious, filling, I know exactly what's gone into them and a batch will last a few weeks!*

*If you can keep them hidden from yourself, that is. Speaking from experience.

1. Preheat the oven to 180°C (160°C fan).

2. Mash your sweet potato in a large mixing bowl, then add in your apple, melted butter and honey, if you are using it. Combine everything well.

3. Sift your flour and cinnamon into the bowl and fold the ingredients together with a butter knife. Continue to combine with your hands until you have a dough.

4. On a floured surface, roll out your dough into a long oval, around 1cm thickness. Use a pizza slicer or butter knife to cut out your bars. I make mine around 8cm long and 2cm wide. Repeat with the rest of the dough until it is all used up.

5. Place your bars onto a tray lined with baking paper, with a small space between each. Bake for 12 minutes, until they've risen slightly and just started to turn colour on top.

6. Transfer to a wire rack to cool. If you're drizzling melted chocolate on top, wait until your bars have cooled completely to do this.

7. Store and freeze to use whenever your little one needs a snack!

What's good:

Sweet potato: rich in iron and vitamin C.

No sneaky added sugars from fruit concentrates.

Rich in fibre: a filling snack.

Graduation (18 months+)

Breakfasts

Lunches

Dinners

Snacks

Special Occasions

Breakfasts

Lunches

Dinners

Snacks

Special Occasions

STAGE

5

Stage 5: Graduation (18 months+)

From here on out, you're on the road to serving your toddler meals that are exactly the same as the whole family (while still taking things like added salt, sugar and spices into account). The tips on selective eating from the previous chapter may be more relevant than ever, as your little one continues to stretch their independence muscles and add to their ever-growing bank of opinions! Biologically, your toddler isn't growing as much now as they were in their infancy, so if their appetite seems smaller, this can be why. The amount they eat can vary wildly from one day to the next as they experience growth spurts, fussier days and days where they are burning more energy. Continue to take their lead and try to keep these rules in mind if things get challenging:

Play the cards you're dealt

Toddlers are all about independence, autonomy, choice and testing boundaries. Play to your strengths and allow them elements of these things when it comes to food.

- Give them a sense of choice over what they eat. This doesn't mean they get free rein over the menu, but rather you give them a choice of two healthy options and allow them to pick which they're going to eat. Even better if you can physically show them the foods and allow them to select one (this obviously isn't always possible with cooked meals, but a visual will help).

- If there is no choice, give them a heads-up of what's coming, 'This afternoon, we're going to the shops and then we're going to have spaghetti Bolognese for dinner.' This allows them to get their head around the idea of the meal before being presented with it.

- Try to avoid all-day grazing. In order for your toddler to continue to develop intuitive eating they need to experience those feelings of hunger and fullness. If their belly is always somewhat topped up from snacking or drinking milk, they are going to feel more empowered to refuse a meal. Let hunger be the persuasive factor that gets them involved in what you're serving them.

- Keep steering clear of highly processed snacks, junk food, crisps, cereal bars, etc. These are full of empty calories and take up valuable space in their tummies.

Less is more

- If your little one is in a particularly selective phase, keep their servings small and manageable. Small portions can be less overwhelming, which can really help with taking the pressure off at mealtimes. They also provide the opportunity for your little one to ask for more, which they will do if they still feel hungry.

Don't negotiate with terrorists!

In our worry and desire to get them eating, we parents can often resort to foolish measures. The bottom line is, mealtimes should never be seen as a negotiation!

▶ Don't push, bribe or bargain. Pudding or treats should never be used as a reward or bargaining chip to get your little one to have 'one more bite'. Instead, offer them their meal and if you are planning to follow up with a dessert, such as fruit or frozen yoghurt, you can wait and see how the meal unfolds without mentioning it to them at all. If they finish the majority of their meal you can offer dessert, but if they aren't engaging much, take that as a sign they are not all that hungry and save dessert for another day.

▶ If you offer a meal, set a time limit (20 to 30 minutes is usually sufficient for this age group) and if nothing is eaten you can simply take the meal away. You don't need to make a big song and dance about this, or communicate anything that suggests you're emotional or disappointed that they haven't eaten. It's simply you saying, 'I can see you're not interested in eating right now', and drawing a line under it for now.

▶ Don't narrow the choice of what you offer. When we do this, we are enabling our toddler to get 'stuck' within a limited diet, and it can be very difficult to get them unstuck! Keep offering a wide variety of foods, flavours and textures. Balance their plate so there are accepted foods alongside new foods, or foods that have the potential to be refused.

▶ Try not to let them know you are bothered by them not eating. Toddlers are almost constantly playing a game of, 'If I do this, what is the reaction?' and when we give attention to specific behaviours, we can inadvertently cause them to happen more regularly.

▶ Don't force an empty plate. Remember, meals are an opportunity to eat, not an expectation to eat.

Let it go

You can't control everything, and trying to will only put undue pressure on the situation and make mealtimes feel unpleasant and anxiety-inducing.

★ If they do skip a meal or snack (due to not wanting to eat), that is okay! They won't starve and at the next mealtime they will likely make up for it.

★ Try to resist predicting or assuming how a meal will go – for example, 'I won't bother putting that on her plate because she won't eat it.' Instead, if you suspect a food will be refused, you can serve tiny amounts on the plate alongside other known and accepted foods. If it's ignored, rejected or removed from the plate, don't draw any particular attention to it.

Blueberry Swirls

20 mins   15 mins

VG   DF   NF

Makes 8 swirls

100g blueberries
4 apricot halves
3 tbsp ground golden flaxseed
1 sheet ready-made puff pastry
1 beaten egg

A scoop of full-fat yoghurt,
   to serve

Fridge: 3 days
Freezer: up to 3 months
Freezing method: freezer bag

**What's
good:**

Blueberry and apricot:
natural sweetness and
rich in vitamins.

Flaxseed: protein-rich and
packed with omega 3s for
brain development.

Who can resist a little continental breakfast? Although we unfortunately can't start every day with a pastry, it is definitely a wonderful treat when we can! These little swirls are a delight – full of the natural sweetness of blueberry and apricot, wrapped in flaky swirls of puff pastry. They're bound to be a hit and can also be offered as a snack. My trusty ground flaxseed not only boosts the protein and nutrient content, but is also key to thickening the filling for the pastries. You could use a few teaspoons of chia seeds to thicken the fruit as an alternative, but the mixture will take longer to thicken (30 minutes to 2 hours) and chia seeds do not retain their nutrients once cooked. It will also make the swirls higher in fibre, which isn't advised for under-twos. For those reasons, I'd recommend sticking to flaxseed for this one.

1. In a blender, whizz together your blueberries and apricots.

2. Add the ground flaxseed to the blended fruit, stir well, then refrigerate for 15 minutes to allow it to thicken.

3. Preheat the oven according to the instructions on your puff pastry and take your pastry out of the fridge.

4. When the fruit gel has thickened, roll out your puff pastry and spread an even layer of fruit gel across the sheet. If you have any fruit gel left over, pop it in an airtight tub in the fridge and use it as a topping for yoghurt or porridge.

5. At this stage you could simply roll up the pastry into a Swiss roll and cut it into pinwheels, or make swirls.

6. For swirls, have your puff pastry portrait in front of you (so the shortest edge faces away from you). Imagine it is in thirds. Fold the bottom third up over the 'middle' third, then the top third down over that middle third (so you have 3 layers folded on top of each other). Use a pizza slicer to cut it into 8 equal strips. Take a strip and gently twist it (as if you're making pastry twists). Place the twist down on a flat surface, use your thumb to hold the end of the twist in place and gently circle it around itself to form a spiral. Pinch the ends of the pastry together to close the spiral. This gives you one completed swirl. Repeat with the remaining swirls.

7. Place your pinwheels or swirls onto a lined baking tray, with about ½cm gap to encourage them to rise upwards. Brush with the beaten egg.

8. Cook according to the instructions on your puff pastry.

9. Serve with a scoop of full-fat yoghurt (or dairy-free alternative).

Lentil Loaf

10 mins   40 mins

VG   DF

Makes 1 loaf

200g cooked brown lentils,
   drained and rinsed
2 medium overripe bananas,
   plus extra slices for topping
1 egg
1 tsp vanilla extract
1 tbsp almond butter
2 tsp lemon juice
50g jumbo porridge oats
100g plain flour
1 tsp bicarbonate of soda
Grated apple, banana slices
   or berries for topping
   (optional)

Drizzle of almond butter and
   some fresh berries, to serve

Airtight container: 2 days
Fridge: 4 days
Freezer: up to 3 months
Freezing method: cut into
   slices and wrap each in
   cling film

Lentils are most often seen as a savoury option, but they certainly lend themselves well to this breakfast loaf. It's subtly sweet with some earthiness, which makes it super versatile when you come to serve it – you could offer it as it is with some fresh berries and yoghurt, or even lightly toast the loaf and spread with some unsalted butter.

Removing everything from the food processor and doing the majority of the mixing by hand ensures that air gets into the batter, which results in a better rise. You can do everything in the food processor if you'd prefer – your loaf will just be more dense!

1. Preheat the oven to 190°C (170°C fan). Grease or line a 450g loaf tin.

2. In a food processor or strong blender, blitz your lentils and bananas together. You can also mash them by hand, but you will have chunkier lentils in your final loaf.

3. Transfer your banana-lentil mixture to a large mixing bowl and add the egg, vanilla extract, almond butter and lemon juice and combine.

4. Fold your oats and flour into the mixture. When it's almost combined, add in the bicarbonate of soda and fold the ingredients together into a smooth batter.

5. Pour the batter into the loaf tin. Top with grated apple or other fresh fruit, such as banana slices or berries.

6. Bake for 30–40 minutes or until a skewer comes out clean. Leave to cool in the tin on a wire rack before turning out.

7. Serve 1–2 slices of lentil loaf topped with an added drizzle of almond butter and some fresh berries.

What's good:

Lentils: a good source of iron, fibre, folate and plant-based protein.

Potassium-rich: supports heart health and the circulatory system.

Breakfast Roll Ups

10 mins   10 mins

VG   NF

Makes 1–2 baby portions

Olive oil, for frying
1 small red pepper, finely
    chopped
A handful of finely chopped
    leek
2 eggs
20g grated cheese
1 mini tortilla wrap

Fresh fruit and a dollop of
    plain yoghurt, to serve

Fridge: up to 3 days
Freezer: up to 3 months
Freezing method: flash
    freeze, then transfer
    to a freezer bag

These roll ups are not only a great breakfast but also a fab meal for any time of the day. Nutritious, great for self-feeding and a fun twist on omelettes, they give little ones lots to explore in terms of shape, flavour and hidden colours and textures. The veggie options are endless, but I particularly like using some juicy red pepper and a little handful of leek, whose mildly oniony flavour profile is less sharp than a spring onion, but brings that same punch of freshness that works so well with eggs. Start with a small amount on first offering and see how your little one reacts!

1. In a small frying pan over a medium heat, add some oil and then add your red pepper and leek. Stir for a few minutes until the leeks begin to soften.

2. Crack your eggs into a bowl and whisk, then pour them into the pan over the veggies. Ensure all the veggies are incorporated in the egg mixture.

3. Sprinkle the grated cheese over the top of your egg, then place your tortilla wrap on top. Leave to cook for 2–3 minutes.

4. Run a spatula around the underside/outside of the egg mixture, then turn the pan over onto a plate, before transferring back to the pan, wrap side down and egg side up. Cook for a further minute to toast the wrap slightly.

5. Roll up the wrap into a cylinder shape, then cut into spiral slices.

6. Serve with fresh fruit and a dollop of plain yoghurt.

What's good:

Tortilla wrap: fortified with iron and great for easy self-feeding.

Leek: rich in flavonoids and antioxidants, which are anti-inflammatory.

Red pepper: rich in vitamin C to aid iron absorption.

Chicken Sausage Rolls

20 mins   35 mins

DF   NF

Makes 8 sausage rolls

6 chicken chipolatas
   (approximately 240g of
   chicken sausage-meat)
½ courgette, peeled and grated
½ onion, diced
3 tbsp flaxseed
1–2 tsp dried oregano
1 sheet of ready-made puff
   pastry
1 beaten egg
Hulled sesame seeds, for
   sprinkling
Black pepper, for sprinkling

Dipping sauce and some
   slices of crunchy red
   pepper, to serve

Fridge: 3 days
Freezer: up to 2 months
Freezing method: in a
   freezer bag. Defrost
   in the fridge overnight

A picnic classic, sausage rolls are great for lunches and also ideal for on-the-go. These chicken versions are lower in salt than a traditional pork sausage, so much more suitable for little ones. Add some hidden veggies and wrap it up in flaky puff pastry and you are onto a winner!

1. Preheat the oven to 200°C (180°C fan).

2. Remove the skin from your chipolatas and add the meat to a large mixing bowl. Add in your courgette, onion, flaxseed and oregano. Mix together by hand.

3. Roll out your puff pastry and cut it in half lengthways, so you have one long rectangle at the top and another at the bottom. These will form two separate rolls.

4. To construct one roll, focus on just the top rectangle of puff pastry. Brush this with beaten egg. Take half of the sausage filling and spread it across the length of the bottom half of your rectangle, leaving a gap of 1cm from any edge. Brush the edges with some more beaten egg, then fold the top half of the rectangle over the filling. Press down the edges with the prongs of a fork.

5. Repeat the process for the bottom rectangle of your puff pastry, using up the remainder of your sausage filling.

6. Brush the tops of your constructed sausage rolls with beaten egg, then sprinkle on some sesame seeds and black pepper.

7. Cut each long sausage roll into smaller portion sizes. I like to cut them in half, then half again to create 8 sausage rolls around 10cm in length each.

8. Place on a baking paper lined tray and cook for 30–35 minutes.

9. Serve with a dipping sauce (see page 194) and some slices of crunchy red pepper.

What's good:

Chicken sausage: lower in salt than traditional pork sausages.

Courgette: vitamin C and antioxidants.

Spring Greens Mini Quiches

30 mins   25 mins

VG   NF

Makes 10–12 mini quiches

100g unsalted butter, cut into
    cubes, plus extra for greasing
50g asparagus, finely chopped
50g frozen peas, finely chopped
½ tsp garlic granules
1 tbsp lemon juice
4 eggs
2 tbsp milk
200g plain flour, plus extra
    for dusting
50g grated cheese

Fridge: 3 days
Freezer: up to 3 months
Freezing method: once
    entirely cooled, wrap
    individually in cling film
    and then freeze

These are a really fun, fresh and filling lunch option. When I think of quiche, I'm thinking of a late spring/early summer lunch in the sunshine vibe. Picky plates with a little side salad. That's why I love using asparagus and garden peas in this recipe as the flavours work so nicely together and give a real springtime punch. But at any other time of year, a substitution of whatever veggies are in season would be just as delicious!

1. Preheat the oven to 200°C (180°C fan). Grease the holes of a 12-hole muffin tin with butter.

2. Add the asparagus and peas to a bowl, then add your garlic granules and lemon juice to the veggies, mix well and leave to sit.

3. Add your eggs and milk to a jug, whisk together and leave to one side while you make your crust.

4. In a large mixing bowl, add your cubed butter and flour. Rub the butter into the flour by hand until it resembles fine breadcrumbs. This can take a good few minutes. Add 2 tablespoons of water and bring it together by hand until it forms a dough. Add another 1–2 tablespoons of water if you feel it is needed to hold it together.

5. On a floured surface, roll out your dough to ½cm thickness. Use a glass or cookie cutter, around 8cm in diameter, to cut out 10–12 rounds of dough.

6. Take each round of dough and gently press them into the muffin tin, taking care to create a dip without breaking the dough.

7. Fill each tartlet halfway with the egg mixture. Add 1 tablespoon of veggies to each, and then top up with egg until the mixture is almost filling the dough casing.

8. Top each mini quiche with a sprinkle of grated cheese before baking for 20–25 minutes.

What's good:

A complete meal!

Peas: plant-based protein and iron.

Asparagus: contains asparagine, which is anti-inflammatory and helps the body flush out toxins and excess salt.

Lentil Dahl

15 mins   35 mins

V   VG   DF   GF   NF

Makes 2 adult portions and
2 baby portions, or 8 baby
portions

Olive oil, for frying
1 onion, finely diced
1 tsp ground cumin
1 tsp garam masala
1 tsp smoked paprika
200g split red lentils, rinsed
1 x 400g tin of chopped
    tomatoes
1 small courgette, peeled and
    chopped
50g Tenderstem broccoli,
    finely chopped
1 tin of full-fat coconut milk
A handful of spinach (optional)

Flatbread, sliced red pepper
    and plain yoghurt, to serve

Fridge: 4 days
Freezer: up to 3 months
Freezing method: in
    portions in freezer bags

On those days where the fridge is bare and a trip to the shops just isn't going to happen, this dahl is ideal. Made up of cupboard staples (and an onion), it's great to be able to throw together something that is still wholesome, nutritious and yummy! I love this method of cooking the lentils in coconut milk as the result is creamy, slightly sweet with hints of coconut and works perfectly with the curry spices.

Lots of veggies also work well in this dish if you have some to throw in – grated carrot, potato or sweet potato, greens and even thinly sliced red pepper all bring a nice veggie twist. We usually eat it with a handful of spinach thrown in and some of my homemade flatbreads (page 156).

1. In a large saucepan, over a medium heat, add some olive oil and the diced onion. Allow it to cook for a minute or two, then add in your spices, stirring well to mix with the onion and bring out the flavours.

2. Put your lentils in a sieve and give them a thorough rinse. Add the chopped tomatoes, lentils and veggies to the pan, continually stirring to combine everything with the spices.

3. Pour over your coconut milk and stir well. Bring it to the boil, before reducing the heat right down to allow it to simmer. Cook for 25–35 minutes, stirring at regular intervals to ensure no lentils are sticking to the pan.

4. When you have around 15 minutes of cooking time left, mix in your handful of spinach, if using.

5. You can add a splash of water if you feel it's drying out, but once the lentils are soft and the liquid has reduced, your dahl is ready!

6. Serve a couple of wooden spoonfuls with some flatbread, sliced red pepper and yoghurt on the side.

What's good:

Cooked spinach: full of non-haem iron and calcium.

Lentils: high-quality protein.

Coconut milk: iron-rich and good for digestion.

Brown Stew Chicken

20 mins   2+ hours   50 mins

DF   NF   GF

Makes 2 adult portions and 2 baby portions

75g dried pitted prunes (or prune purée pouch)
500g skinless and boneless chicken thigh fillets, chopped into 2cm chunks
1 tsp garlic powder or crushed garlic
1 tsp smoked paprika
1 tsp dried thyme
¼ tsp allspice
2.5cm chunk of fresh ginger, chopped
1 red pepper, finely chopped
2 shallots, finely chopped
3 spring onions, finely chopped
2 tbsp olive oil
2 tbsp ketchup
400ml baby-friendly chicken stock
1 Scotch bonnet (or milder chillies if desired)
1 tbsp brown sugar (for adult portions)

Optional – to cook your rice in your stew, add:
250g rice

Fridge: 2 days
Freezer: up to 3 months
Freezing method: portion into freezer bags

A traditional Caribbean dish, brown stew chicken is homely, filling and very delicious! It's normally made with a lot of brown sugar and/or browning (molasses), which would be far too sugary for little ones. This recipe is my adaptation, using prunes and opting for sweeter veggies such as shallots instead of regular onions to bring the sweetness to the dish. Marinating your chicken overnight will yield the best results, it is a labour of love but oh-so-worth it!

I like to add some Scotch bonnets, and leaving them whole in the stew keeps the overall infusion of heat quite mild and subtle. (look out for them to avoid putting a whole one on someone's plate though!). Remember, there's no reason not to experiment with heat in your little one's food, and this dish is a great opportunity for it. You can also use milder chillies if this is one of the first times you have experimented with heat in their food.

1. Place the dried prunes in a small heatproof bowl and soak them in just-boiled water for 15 minutes. Once soaked, blend them into a purée. You can use some of the water used for soaking to thin out the consistency of the purée slightly.

2. In a large mixing bowl, add your chicken, garlic, paprika, thyme, allspice and chopped ginger. Mix well, using your hands to rub the spices into the chicken meat. Add in your prune purée, pepper, shallots and spring onions and mix well. Cover and leave the chicken to marinate in the fridge for at least 2 hours, but overnight is even better.

3. Before cooking, remove the chicken from the fridge and allow it to sit at room temperature for 15 minutes. Putting chicken straight from the fridge to the pan gives a higher chance you will end up with dry chicken, and nobody wants that!

4. To cook the stew, heat 2 tablespoons oil in a large pan over a medium heat. Lift the chicken pieces from the mixing bowl and fry them for 10–15 minutes, turning regularly until cooked through.

5. Add in any remaining marinade, onions and pepper left in the bowl, as well as your chicken stock and ketchup, and stir well. If using Scotch bonnets, add them whole into the pan at this point. Bring it to the boil, then reduce the heat, cover and cook for a further 35 minutes, stirring regularly.

6. You might like to cook rice separately for this dish, but I often add it into the stew itself. If you do want to do this, simply stir in the rice with an extra 120ml of water, 15 minutes before the end of cooking time. As the rice cooks, you can add more water in small quantities if you feel it needs it.

Lots of spices to explore new flavours.

Chicken thigh: dark meat with higher quantities of iron and zinc.

7. Once your rice has cooked and your stew is reduced, it's time to serve. You can separate adult and baby portions and stir 1 tablespoon brown sugar into adult portions if you want to. It's a filling dish, so your little one will only need a few tablespoons.

Lamb Koftas in Flatbread

20 mins   15 mins

NF

Makes 8 koftas

1 tbsp olive oil
2 shallots, diced
1 crushed garlic clove or 1 tsp
   garlic powder
250g lamb mince
A few leaves of mint, finely
   chopped
1 tbsp plain yoghurt

Roasted Mediterranean
   veggies, to serve

Per flatbread:
60g Greek yoghurt
50g self-raising flour, plus
   extra for dusting

Fridge: 2 days
Freezer: up to 2 months
Freezing method: these can
   be frozen before or after
   cooking. Wrap each kofta
   individually in foil or
   cling film and then freeze

These koftas are always a hit in our house! Lamb and mint is a dreamy flavour combo. Add to that sweet, caramelised shallots, tangy yoghurt dressing and a doughy flatbread and you have a seriously moreish meal. This is a great one to enjoy together as a family – your little one will watch with interest to see how you tackle the flatbread. It's a great opportunity to model to them how to pick it up, hold it together and take a bite with all the fillings. But don't worry if they'd rather pick it apart and eat it deconstructed style, it's all part of the fun and exploration!

1. In a pan with a little of the oil, add your shallots and cook until they begin to soften and caramelise. Add in your garlic and cook for a further minute or so, then remove the pan from the heat and leave the onions and garlic to cool.

2. In a mixing bowl, add your lamb mince, three-quarters of the mint, a small splash of oil and your onion and garlic mix. Combine everything well.

3. Shape your koftas – you can go for traditional skewer shapes or flatter, more patty-like koftas. Wet hands will keep the mixture from sticking to you.

4. There are many cooking options to choose from here! These are a great air fryer option (180°C for around 10 minutes, turning regularly), but they can also be cooked on a griddle pan or in the oven (200°C/180°C fan for around 15 minutes, turning over halfway). However you cook them, leave the lamb to rest for around 5 minutes once cooked and then they are ready to serve.

5. While your koftas cook, in a mixing bowl combine the Greek yoghurt and flour. Bring it together until it forms a dough, but don't over-knead it.

6. On a lightly floured surface, use a rolling pin to shape it into a flat circle, around ½cm thick.

7. Heat a pan over a medium heat. Wait for the pan to be heated before popping your flatbread in. Dry fry the flatbread (no oil) for 2–3 minutes on each side, until brown patches appear. Tear a small piece of the bread to check it is cooked through, if not, allow it a few more minutes on each side.

8. For your yoghurt dressing, take a small bowl and add the 1 tablespoon of yoghurt, the remainder of your mint and a tiny splash of water. Mix together well.

9. Pop a lamb kofta inside a flatbread and drizzle the yoghurt dressing on top (or serve on the side to dip). Serve with some roasted Mediterranean veggies!

What's good:

Lamb: rich in zinc, vitamin B12 and haem iron (which is more easily absorbed by the body).

Mint: nutrient-rich, good for digestion, and a fun, fresh new flavour for your little one to enjoy.

Koftas: easy self-feeding and a good way to incorporate meat into their diet.

Easy Peasy Mac & Cheese

10 mins   45 mins

VG   NF

Makes 4 adult portions and 2 baby portions

275g macaroni
400ml milk or milk alternative
1 tsp onion powder
½ tbsp yellow mustard
100g veggies – kale, grated
    courgette, grated carrot,
    peas, broccoli or cauliflower
200g cheese, grated
Approx 50g breadcrumbs
    (1 slice, blended)
A few handfuls of baby-
    friendly cheese puffs
    (optional)*

*Look for options marketed to babies, or with a lower salt content.

Fridge: 3 days
Freezer: up to 3 months
Freezing method: in
    portions in tubs or bags

A great one for all the family, this mac & cheese is my one-pot solution. The method is a little bit like the hokey cokey (in, out, in, out, stir it all about) but ultimately that's the trade-off for managing to do it all in one roasting dish, rather than the more focus-intensive, traditional method of boiling your pasta and making up your cheese sauce separately, then combining it all together. If you can get your prep out the way earlier in the day (peeling veggies, grating cheese, blending breadcrumbs and cheese puffs), then the remainder of the cooking is actually quite simple and will just require you to reset a 10-minute timer a few times over until the dish is done!

Cheese does contain higher levels of salt, so just be mindful of the options you choose and the amount you add in. I find 200g is just enough to create a tasty, comforting, indulgent dish. I use a mixture of mature Cheddar for cheesiness and mozzarella or Gruyère for that satisfying stringy pull! The crispy cheese puff topping adds an extra layer of deliciousness!

1. Preheat the oven to 200°C (180°C fan).

2. Add your macaroni to a casserole or roasting dish. Spread it into an even layer across the bottom. Pour in your milk and 400ml of water, add your onion powder and mustard.

3. Stir everything well, ensuring as much of the macaroni is submerged as possible. Some might still stick out of the liquid but that's okay, as it will be moved around and rotated into the liquid at each stirring interval.

4. Pop your dish into the oven for 20 minutes, stirring halfway through. Make sure you get round the edges/corners of the dish to really move the pasta around.

5. Remove your dish from the oven and add in your veggies, mixing well. If you feel like you need to add more water at this point you can, but don't add too much. Pop it back in the oven for another 10 minutes.

6. Take the dish out, add in the cheese and stir well. Return it to the oven for another 10 minutes.

7. This is the final interval! Remove your dish from the oven, stir it well, then sprinkle your breadcrumbs and cheese puffs on top if you like. Return the dish to the oven for 5 more minutes to allow this top layer to crisp up.

8. Serve a few tablespoons on their own with some fresh fruit, or add as a side to cooked chicken. This is a filling dish, so your little one won't need a huge portion!

Banana Oat Muffins

10 mins   20 mins

VG   NF

Makes 12 muffins

2 overripe bananas
1 large egg
100ml milk
30g unsalted butter, melted
25g Greek or plain yoghurt
60g rolled oats
40g ground flaxseed
100g plain flour
1 tsp baking powder
½ tsp bicarbonate of soda
Toppings – banana slices,
    grated apple or chopped
    blueberries (optional)

Airtight container in fridge:
    4 days
Airtight container: 2 days
Freezer: up to 3 months
Freezing method: in a
    freezer bag or plastic
    wrap. Defrost at room
    temperature for 1–2
    hours or microwave for
    30 seconds, turning over
    halfway

Whenever I make snacks for Rue, especially yummy baked goods, there's a little something I like to call 'Mum Tax' (substitute as appropriate: Dad Tax, Grandparent Tax... any other caregiver Tax). This tax comes in the form of a certain proportion being eaten by me. I know I won't be alone in this. We can pretend this is done purely in the name of quality checking, but we all know it's more to do with the fact that we too deserve some deliciousness in our lives! And we're probably running on leftovers, so we need a little boost of calories now and then.

Long story short, these are one of my favourite snacks for levying a heavy Mum Tax. And by that I mean at least three muffins are reserved for me. They're delicious, packed full of healthy energy sources and also have a good dose of protein. These are great as a snack, a breakfast, and because both oats and bananas are rich in magnesium, potassium and tryptophan (which all contribute to healthy sleep), they even make a good before-bed snack.

1. Preheat the oven to 200°C (180°C fan). Line a 12-hole muffin tin with silicone or paper cupcake cases.

2. In a large mixing bowl, mash your bananas, then add the egg, milk, unsalted butter and yoghurt and mix together.

3. In a second mixing bowl, add your oats, flaxseed, flour, baking powder and bicarbonate of soda and combine.

4. Gradually fold your dry ingredients into the wet ingredients to form a batter.

5. Divide the batter equally into the muffin cases. You could also add toppings to each, if you like. Bake for 15–20 minutes, until a skewer inserted in the centre comes out clean. Leave to cool on a wire rack.

6. Serve on their own as a snack, or with some cheese chunks and fresh fruit as a breakfast alternative!

What's good:

Flaxseed: omega 3s for brain development and fibre to support healthy digestion.

Oats: fortified with iron and a rich source of energy.

Banana Coco Chocolate Cookies

10 mins   18 mins

V   VG   GF   DF   NF

Makes 10 cookies

1 overripe banana
45–50g desiccated coconut
½ tbsp unsweetened cocoa
   or cacao powder

Airtight container at room
   temp: 2 days
Fridge: up to 5 days

These cookies feel like cheating because they are so ridiculously simple to make. They are also a great first recipe to use for baking together with your little one – they will love getting involved with mashing, mixing and measuring! And as this recipe doesn't use any egg, sneaky little tastes of the cookie dough are more than fine!

1. Preheat the oven to 200°C (180°C fan). Line a baking tray with baking paper.

2. In a large bowl, mash your banana well. Mix in the desiccated coconut until everything is well combined, then stir in the cocoa or cacao powder. The cookie dough should hold together and be sticky – if it seems too wet add small amounts of coconut at a time and stir well.

3. Use a tablespoon measure to scoop up the dough, press it into the measure and level off the top. Turn the tablespoon measure over on the tray and tap the cookie onto the baking paper, then flatten it into a circle with a fork.

4. Bake for 15–18 minutes, until slightly crisp around the edges.

What's good:

Banana and cacao: potassium-rich for healthy body and brain function.

A fun bake-together recipe.

Egg, gluten and dairy free!

Dips

Here are some of my favourite baby-friendly dipping sauces! Scale measurements up or down depending on how much you need, but any extra will last in the fridge in an airtight container for 3–5 days.

SAVOURY

A great accompaniment to tots, nuggets, fritters or just about anything!

2.   BBQ (V VG GF NF DF)

Same as Tomato dip but adjust to ½ tbsp tomato purée with 1½ tbsp of prune purée and add in a sprinkle of smoked paprika.

1.   Tomato (V VG GF NF DF)

In a pan, heat a dash of olive oil. Add 1 tbsp of tomato purée and 1 tbsp prune purée. Mix together gently over the heat until combined.

3.   Smoky Tahini Dip (V VG GF NF DF)

Take 2 tbsp tahini, ½ tsp lemon juice, ½ tsp olive oil, a sprinkle of garlic powder and a sprinkle of smoked paprika. Mix together. Gradually stir in 1 to 2 tbsp of warm water to your desired consistency.

4.   Fresh Yoghurty Dip (VG NF GF)

Yoghurt alone makes a fantastic dip for little ones, but you can also add some finely grated cucumber (remove the watery seeded middle first) and/or some finely chopped mint for a cool, refreshing variation.

5. Cheese & Chive (VG GF NF)

Add 3 tbsp cottage cheese with a small handful of chopped chives to a blender and blend to a smooth consistency.

6. Curried Carrot Dip (V VG GF NF DF)

Peel and roast a large carrot until soft, and blend into a puree with a tbsp water and ½ tsp of curry powder.

SWEET

A fun treat for dipping fruits and breadsticks or spreading on toast.

1. Chocolate Nut Butter (V VG GF DF)

Mix ½ tsp cocoa powder with 2 tbsp cashew butter. Add in a small drizzle of vegetable oil if you would like a runnier consistency.

2. Cream Cheese (VG GF NF)

Mix 1 tbsp cream cheese with 1 tbsp pureed or mashed fruit of your choice – strawberries, pineapple and mango all work nicely! You can also add in a few drops of vanilla extract for added flavour.

Baby-Friendly Easter Brownies

15 mins   30 mins

VG   DF   NF

Makes 16 brownies

1 Medjool date, stoned, or
    2 tbsp blended raisins, to
    sweeten
450g steamed sweet potato
    (approx. 2 large sweet
    potatoes)
2 eggs
2 tsp vanilla extract
170g plain flour
40g unsweetened cacao powder
2 tsp ground cinnamon
1 tsp baking powder

Airtight container at room
    temp: 2 days
Fridge: 4 days
Freezer: up to 3 months
Freezing method: in a
    freezer bag or tub.
    Separate each brownie
    with baking paper

I loved making these at Easter for Rue to enjoy something chocolatey. As much as it's nice to treat little ones to the real thing every now and then, it's also great to have more nutritious options to fall back on that give them the same joy. These brownies are chocolatey, fudgey, moreish, and tick all the boxes for offering your little one a delicious treat!

1. Preheat the oven to 180°C (160°C fan). In a square roasting dish, use a rectangle of baking paper to line the bottom, with some extra length at the edges to help you remove the brownie once it's cooked.

2. Soak your date or raisins in a heatproof bowl of just-boiled water for 5 minutes, then blend them together with your steamed sweet potato.

3. In a large mixing bowl, combine this mixture together with your eggs and vanilla extract. Add your flour, cacao, cinnamon and baking powder and fold together.

4. Pour your brownie batter into the lined dish and spread evenly. Bake the brownie for 25–30 minutes, until the top has darkened and a skewer inserted into the centre comes out clean.

5. Leave the brownie to cool for 5–10 minutes, then remove it from the dish and cut into 16 equal brownies.

What's good:

Sweet potato: iron, vitamin C and natural sweetness.

Cacao: iron, potassium, protein and fibre.

Less sugar and more nutrient-rich than traditional brownies.

Festive Mince Pie Tarts

40 mins   15 mins

VG   NF

Makes 12–15 tarts

1 Medjool date, stoned*
50g raisins*
1 small apple, peeled and
  grated
1 small carrot, peeled and
  grated
Juice and pulp of ½ orange
1 tsp vanilla extract
1 tsp allspice
2 tsp ground cinnamon
1 egg, beaten
1 tbsp ground flaxseed
1 sheet ready-made puff pastry

Full-fat plain yoghurt, to serve

*Use less of these ingredients
to reduce the sugar content.

Airtight container: 2 days
Fridge: 4 days
Freezer: up to 3 months
Freezing method: flash
  freeze, then transfer
  to a freezer bag or tub

These tarts will give your little one a taste of traditional, delicious Christmas spices all while making your house smell incredible as you're cooking them! Dates and raisins are used to sweeten this recipe, and while they do add sugar there is no reason to be afraid of these ingredients in moderation. Both dates and raisins are a rich source of iron and potassium, so they bring their own benefits to this recipe. For some added festive cheer, sprinkle some desiccated coconut over your tarts for 'snow'!

1. In a shallow heatproof bowl, add your date, raisins and enough just-boiled water to submerge them. Leave them to soak for 5–10 minutes.

2. Preheat the oven to 200°C (180°C fan).

3. In a saucepan over a medium-low heat, add all of your ingredients except the flaxseed and puff pastry. Drain the dates and raisins before adding them, as the extra liquid won't be needed. Allow the ingredients to gently cook and soften, stirring regularly, for 10–15 minutes.

4. Once softened, mix in the ground flaxseed. I leave my filling chunky, but you could use a hand blender at this stage to further blitz up the texture of the filling if desired.

5. Roll out your puff pastry and use a cookie cutter, glass or knife to cut out shapes that will form the bases of your tarts.

6. Spread around 1 tablespoon of filling on each tart, leaving a gap around the perimeter of each. Brush the edge of each tart with beaten egg. If you have any leftover filling, refrigerate (or freeze!) it once cooled and use as a festive breakfast or yoghurt topper. You could even use it to make some Christmassy yoghurt bark (see page 112)!

7. Place your tarts on a baking tray lined with baking paper and cook for 12–15 minutes, or until the edges are golden and the pastry is cooked.

8. Serve 1–2 tarts as a snack with some full-fat plain yoghurt.

What's good:
New festive flavours to explore.

Dates and raisins: rich in iron, soluble fibre and potassium.

Spiced Pumpkin Muffins

1 hour · 25 mins

Makes 12 muffins

1 large pumpkin
180g plain flour
½ tsp grated nutmeg
1 tsp ground cinnamon
1 tsp bicarbonate of soda
1 egg
1 tsp lemon juice
1 tsp vanilla extract
125ml milk
2 tbsp coconut oil, melted
Around 30g peanut butter

Yoghurt sprinkled with
  cinnamon and grated
  carrot, to serve

Airtight container: 2 days
Fridge: 4 days
Freezer: up to 3 months
Freezing method: flash
  freeze, then transfer to a
  freezer bag or tub

Whether you're getting in the pumpkin spiced latte spirit or feeling spooky for Halloween, you can't avoid the abundance of pumpkins around you during the autumn months. The unfortunate thing about pumpkins is that a lot of them go to waste, despite being packed with antioxidants and vitamins! They are a great food for weaning because they have a very mild taste and can be mixed into many different dishes – including these spiced pumpkin muffins. These have all the warming flavours of autumn and can be offered as a breakfast, snack or on-the-go meal.

1. Preheat the oven to 200°C (180°C fan). Line a 12-hole muffin tin with silicone or paper cupcake cases.

2. Cut your pumpkin in half and scoop out all of the seeds and stringy bits (you could save the seeds and roast them if you want to make use of them!). Place the pumpkin on a baking tray, flesh side up, and roast for around 45 minutes until soft. Leave it to cool (until you can comfortably handle the flesh without burning yourself) before continuing on to the next steps.

3. Reduce the heat of your oven to 190°C (170°C fan).

4. Scoop the flesh out of the roasted pumpkin and use a hand blender or masher to purée it. Transfer the purée to a cheesecloth or muslin cloth and squeeze out the liquid – you may have to do this in batches.

5. You will need 200g of the roasted pumpkin purée for the muffins. Store the remainder in the fridge (for up to 4 days) or the freezer (for up to 3 months) and use it in curries, soups, pasta sauces or more muffins!

6. In a large mixing bowl, add your dry ingredients: flour, nutmeg, cinnamon and bicarbonate of soda.

7. In another bowl, add your wet ingredients: egg, lemon juice, vanilla extract, milk, melted coconut oil and the pumpkin puree.

8. Gently pour your wet ingredients into the dry ingredients, folding them together as you go.

9. Add 1 tablespoon of batter to the bottom of each cupcake case, then add ½ teaspoon of peanut butter, followed by another tablespoon of batter (so the peanut butter is enclosed in the middle of each muffin). Use up the remaining batter equally across your muffins.

10. Bake at 190°C (170°C fan) for 25 minutes, or until a skewer inserted into the centre comes out clean. Leave to cool on a wire rack before serving.

11. Serve with some yoghurt sprinkled with cinnamon and fresh grated carrot.

First Month Of Weaning Plan

Here's an idea of what your first month could look like, with a staggered introduction of allergens. Your baby's first meals can be very hit and miss. You might feel like they're not eating much at all, but remember it's the whole experience of the food that is important. If they are trying an allergen, try to ensure they do eat some of that food in order for you to accurately observe for any reactions.

It's a good idea to start with quite simple, plain tastes of just two or three food items. Over time you will progress to adding in more flavours and textures, until your baby's plates begin to resemble proper meals. Once you're up and running with weaning, turn to page 210 for weekly meal plans including snacks and ready-to-go shopping lists.

Week 1			
	MEAL 1	**MEAL 2**	**ALLERGENS** (new allergens in **bold**)
Mon	1 large floret of softly cooked broccoli 1 adult finger-sized piece of sweet potato* 1 tbsp full-fat plain or Greek **yoghurt** *Cook half of the sweet potato now, and the other half later in the week	n/a	**Dairy**
Tues	¼ of a banana 1 adult finger-sized slice of avocado 1 tbsp full-fat plain or Greek **yoghurt**	n/a	**Dairy**
Weds	A few tbsp porridge, made with whole **cow's milk**, with 1 tsp mashed banana mixed in ½ a steamed pear on the side (in one piece)	n/a	**Dairy**
Thurs	1 finger of **toast** topped with some mashed avocado and a sprinkle of hemp seeds 1 adult finger-sized piece of sweet potato	n/a	**Gluten**

Fri	A few pieces of softly cooked **pasta** 1 large floret of softly cooked broccoli *Optional: stir a tsp of **cream cheese** into the pasta	n/a	**Gluten, Dairy***
Sat	No-Egg Broccoli Tots (page 68) Serve 1 or 2 tots, cut in half lengthways with 1 tbsp plain **yoghurt** ½ a steamed pear (in one piece)	n/a	**Gluten, Dairy**
Sun	1 adult finger-sized piece of grilled chicken (breast or thigh meat) Peas mashed with **milk** 1 adult finger-sized piece of sweet potato	Optional: Make a batch of Low-Allergen Pancakes (page 60) for the freezer. You can make these with whole cow's milk if dairy has been introduced	**Dairy**

Shopping list

Fruit & Veg
1 x broccoli
1 x sweet potato
1 x avocado
1 x pear
1 x banana
Frozen peas

Meat & Fish
Small piece of chicken breast
or thigh

Dairy & Eggs
Tub of full-fat plain or Greek
yoghurt
Optional: cream cheese
Whole cow's milk

Grains & Bread
Oats
Hemp seeds
Sliced bread (low-salt
and soya free until soya is
introduced)
Pasta (white fusilli or personal
preference)

PLUS ingredients for these recipes:
No-Egg Broccoli Tots (page 68)
Optional: Low-Allergen
Pancakes (page 60)

Week 2

	MEAL 1	MEAL 2 (optional at this stage)	ALLERGENS (new allergens in **bold**)
Mon	1 tsp hard-boiled **egg** mashed with milk (include both egg white and yolk) on toast A wedge of grilled red pepper (skin removed)	n/a	Dairy, Gluten, **Egg**
Tues	1 Savoury Muffin (page 80) ½ a golden kiwi, rolled in hemp or ground flaxseed for added grip	n/a	Dairy, Gluten, **Egg**
Weds	1 or 2 finger-sized pieces of cheese omelette (save remainder for Thurs meal 2) 1 or 2 tbsp plain or Greek yoghurt ½ a steamed apple	n/a	Dairy, **Egg**
Thurs	1 Porridge Finger (page 58) ¼ tsp peanut butter mixed into some plain or Greek yoghurt	1 or 2 finger-sized pieces of cheese omelette A wedge of grilled red pepper (skin removed)	Dairy, Egg, **Peanut**
Fri	1 Savoury Muffin (from Tuesday's batch cooking) ½ a golden kiwi, rolled in hemp or ground flaxseed for added grip	1 adult finger-sized, well-cooked beef strip 1 large floret of softly cooked broccoli A small amount of smooth peanut butter from your fingertip	Dairy, Egg, Gluten, **Peanut**
Sat	A small amount of smooth **peanut butter** from your fingertip Toast fingers with a thin layer of mashed banana and a sprinkle of hemp seeds	Mediterranean Chicken (page 72) ½ a steamed apple	Gluten, **Peanut**
Sun	Low-Allergen Pancakes (page 60 or from last week's batch cooking) 1 or 2 tbsp plain or Greek yoghurt	Mediterranean chicken ½ a steamed apple	Dairy

Shopping list

Fruit & Veg
1 x red pepper
1 x golden kiwi
1 x apple
1 x broccoli
1 x banana

Meat & Fish
Small strip of beef

Dairy & Eggs
Tub of full-fat plain or Greek yoghurt
Whole cow's milk
Full-fat Cheddar cheese
2 x eggs

Tinned & Condiments
Peanut butter (smooth, look for options that are 100% peanut)

Grains & Bread
Sliced bread (low-salt and no soya)
Hemp seeds
Ground flaxseed

PLUS ingredients for these recipes:
Savoury Muffins (page 80)
Porridge Fingers (page 58)
Optional:
Mediterranean Chicken (page 72)

Week 3

	MEAL 1	MEAL 2 (begin to introduce this if you haven't already)	ALLERGENS (new allergens in **bold**)
Mon	Low-Allergen Pancakes (from batch) 1 or 2 tbsp plain or Greek yoghurt ½ a steamed plum (in one piece)	Homemade **Houmous** (page 66) With adult finger-sized pieces of steamed carrot and courgette to dip	Dairy, **Sesame**
Tues	1 Porridge Finger (from batch) Small amount of peanut butter mixed into some plain or Greek yoghurt	**Houmous** spread on toast fingers	Dairy, Wheat, Peanut, **Sesame**
Weds	1 or 2 finger-sized pieces of cheese omelette (save remainder) 1 wedge of orange (on the peel, membranes removed)	½ a steamed plum (in one piece)	Egg, Wheat
Thurs	**Houmous** spread on toast fingers 1 wedge of orange (on the peel, membranes removed)	1 adult finger-sized piece of grilled chicken breast or thigh 1 tbsp cooked pasta in Lentil Pasta Sauce (page 64)	Wheat, **Sesame**
Fri	A few tbsp porridge with 1 tsp stewed plum and a sprinkle of hemp seeds mixed in	1 adult finger-sized piece of grilled chicken breast or thigh Adult finger-sized pieces of steamed carrot and courgette	Dairy
Sat	A few tbsp porridge with 1 tsp stewed plum and ¼ tsp peanut butter mixed in	First **Fish** and Chips (page 74) (save a few tbsp of cooked fish)	Peanut, Dairy, **Finned fish**
Sun	Low-Allergen Pancakes (from batch) 2 tbsp plain or Greek yoghurt	1–2 tbsp cooked pasta in Lentil Pasta Sauce with 1 tbsp cooked **fish** mixed in 1 wedge of orange (on the peel, membranes removed)	Dairy, Wheat, **Finned fish**

Shopping list

Fruit & Veg
2 x plum
1 x carrot
1 x courgette
2 x oranges

Dairy & Eggs
Tub of full-fat plain or Greek yoghurt
Whole cow's milk
Full-fat Cheddar cheese
1 x egg

Grains & Bread
Oats
Hemp seeds
Sliced bread (low-salt and no soya)
Pasta (white fusilli or personal preference)

Meat & Fish
2 x small piece of chicken breast or thigh

Tinned & Condiments
Peanut butter (smooth, look for options that are 100% peanut)

PLUS ingredients for these recipes:
Homemade Houmous (page 66)
Lentil Pasta Sauce (page 64)
First Fish and Chips (page 74)

Week 4

	MEAL 1	MEAL 2	MEAL 3 (optional but to work towards)	ALLERGENS (new allergens in **bold**)
Mon	1 Porridge Finger (from batch) Mashed strawberries in some plain or Greek yoghurt **Almond** or **cashew** butter from your fingertip	1 tbsp beef or lamb mince (cook enough for tomorrow) mixed with some mashed avocado 1 adult finger-sized wedge of roasted potato (skin off) Some plain or Greek yoghurt	Cream cheese on toast fingers with a sprinkle of hemp seeds	Dairy, Wheat, **Tree nuts**
Tues	Veggie Scramble (page 82) (save remainder) **Almond** or **cashew** butter from your fingertip 1 large strawberry, squashed slightly	1 tbsp beef or lamb mince mixed with some mashed avocado 1 adult finger-sized wedge of roasted potato (skin off) Almond or cashew butter from your fingertip	Cream cheese with mashed strawberries on toast fingers	Dairy, Wheat, Egg, **Tree nuts**
Weds	Porridge with grated apple and ¼ tsp peanut butter	Veggie Scramble Almond or cashew butter from your fingertip	Veggie Curry (page 70) Yoghurt with some puréed mango	Dairy, Peanut, Egg, **Tree nuts**
Thurs	Chia Jam on Toast (page 62)	Veggie Curry (from batch) 1 adult finger-sized piece of grilled **tofu** 1 adult finger-sized slice of mango rolled in hemp or flaxseed for grip	1–2 tbsp cooked pasta in Lentil Pasta Sauce (from batch)	Wheat, **Soya**
Fri	Porridge with 1 tsp Chia Jam mixed in	No-Egg Broccoli Tots (page 68 or from batch) Serve 1 or 2 tots, cut in half lengthways 1 large strawberry, squashed slightly	Avocado on toast with sprinkle of hemp seeds 1 adult finger-sized piece of grilled **tofu**	Dairy, Wheat, **Soya**

Sat	1 or 2 finger-sized pieces of cheese omelette (save remainder) 1 adult finger-sized slice of mango rolled in hemp or flaxseed for grip	Savoury Muffin (page 80 or from batch) 2 tbsp plain or Greek yoghurt 1 adult finger-sized piece of grilled **tofu**	Low-Allergen pancakes (from batch) spread with some Chia Jam ¼ tsp peanut butter mixed into plain or Greek yoghurt	Dairy, Egg, Wheat, Peanut, **Soya**
Sun	Avocado on toast with sprinkle of hemp seeds Steamed apple	1 adult finger-sized piece of salmon 1 adult finger-sized wedge of roasted potato (skin off) Yoghurt and some puréed mango	1–2 tbsp cooked pasta in Lentil Pasta Sauce (from batch)	Wheat, Finned fish

Shopping list

Fruit & Veg
Strawberries
1 x avocado
1 x potato
1 x apple
1 x mango

Meat & Fish
Beef or lamb mince
1 x salmon fillet

Dairy & Eggs
Tub of full-fat plain or Greek yoghurt
Whole cow's milk
Full-fat Cheddar cheese
1 x egg
Full-fat cream cheese
Tofu

Tinned & Condiments
Peanut butter
Almond or cashew butter (both smooth, look for 100% nut varieties)

Grains & Bread
Sliced bread (low-salt and no soya)
Pasta (white fusilli or personal preference)
Hemp seeds
Ground flaxseed
Oats

PLUS ingredients for these recipes:
Chia Jam (page 62)
Veggie Curry (page 70)
Veggie Scramble (page 82)

Weekly Meal Plans and Shopping Lists

The meals in these plans are suitable from the beginning of weaning, but the schedule itself is aimed at a baby around 12 months, with ideas for three meals a day and a snack. For each week you will find:

- A weekly schedule
- Prep notes to help everything run smoothly
- A shopping list

I've started each week on a Sunday, as this is a day when most people will have a bit more time for food prep.

Where possible, try to eat the same meals or use the same ingredients for the adults in the house too (especially for dinners). This will keep your costs and time in the kitchen down as much as possible! What I haven't included here are any amounts or quantities, as these will differ from family to family. You can make a judgement based on how many people you are feeding, or how many portions you're planning to have left over to freeze!

Shopping list

Fruit & Veg	Meat & Fish	Dairy & Eggs	Grains & Bread
Apple	Chicken thighs	Eggs	Flour
Banana	Salmon (or tinned)	Milk	Oats
Blueberries	Frozen white fish (cod	Cheese	Spaghetti
Broccoli	or pollock)	Full-fat Greek yoghurt	Rice
Cauliflower	Mince (of choice for		Tortilla wraps
Sweet potato (enough	spaghetti)		Sliced bread (low-salt
for pancakes and			and no soya)
wedges)			Chia seeds
Onion	**Spices & Seasoning**	**Tinned & Condiments**	Hemp seeds
Garlic	Cinnamon	Houmous (if not	
Frozen peas	Curry powder	making own)	
	Baby-friendly very	Peanut butter	
	low-salt beef stock (I	Reduced-sugar and	
	recommend Piccolo	-salt baked beans	
	baby-friendly or Kallo	Coconut milk	
	very low salt)	Chopped tomatoes	
		(for Bolognese and for	
		curry)	
		No salt sweetcorn	
		Tomato puree	

Meal Plan 1

DAY	BREAKFAST	LUNCH	DINNER	SNACK
Sunday	Sweet Potato Pancakes (page 88) with Greek yoghurt and blueberries	Broccoli Omelette (page 96)	Chicken thigh fillets with sweet potato wedges and mixed veg	Houmous with red pepper sticks (page 66)
Monday	Porridge with blueberries and peanut butter (page 93)	Houmous chicken wraps (with chicken cooked yesterday)	Salmon Veggie Pancakes (page 102)	One Sweet Potato Pancake with cheese chunks
Tuesday	Porridge with steamed apple and cinnamon (page 93)	Broccoli Omelette (fridge from Sunday)	Salmon Veggie Pancakes (made yesterday)	Houmous on toast strips (page 76)
Wednesday	Scrambled eggs with some tortilla wrap and a side of blueberries	Peanut butter and banana on toast (page 77)	Quesadillas (page 154)	Greek yoghurt with soaked chia seeds and steamed apple
Thursday	Sweet Potato Pancakes with Greek yoghurt and blueberries	Quesadillas (made yesterday)	Fish and Veggie Curry (page 160) with rice	½ banana with cheese chunks
Friday	Peanut butter and banana on toast (page 77)	Fish and Veggie Curry with tortilla wrap	Spaghetti Bolognese (page 106)	Greek yoghurt with soaked chia seeds and blueberries
Saturday	Porridge with banana and almond butter (page 93)	Scrambled eggs with some tortilla wrap and a side of blueberries	Spaghetti Bolognese	One Sweet Potato Pancake (from freezer) with cheese chunks

Prep Notes: these are things you can do in order to prepare for the future meals coming in the week:

Sunday batchcook pancakes, double up portions of omelette and pop the other half in the fridge, set aside some chicken from dinner for tomorrow's lunch and steam an apple and store in the fridge.

Monday batchcook Salmon Veggie Pancakes.

Wednesday double up Quesadillas, store half in fridge once cooled.

Thursday batchcook Fish and Veggie Curry, keep 1 portion in fridge for Friday, freeze the remainder.

Friday batchcook Bolognese, keep 1 portion in fridge for Saturday, freeze the remainder.

Meal Plan 2

DAY	BREAKFAST	LUNCH	DINNER	SNACK
Sunday	Boiled egg* with toast soldiers and half a banana	Pasta with broccoli and cream cheese sauce (page 126)	Lamb Kofta and Flatbread (page 186)	Peanut butter raspberry bites (pop a tiny bit of pb inside each raspberry)
Monday	Cream cheese on toast with raspberries (page 76)	Lamb Kofta with mixed veg	Veggie Chilli (page 132) with crusty bread**	½ banana and cheese chunks
Tuesday	Cinnamon Banana Bites (page 148)	Cream cheese on toast with mango chunks	Veggie Chilli with crusty bread	Peanut butter raspberry bites
Wednesday	Overnight Chia Oats (page 146) with mango	Kidney Bean Burgers (page 98)	Grilled chicken breast, sweet potato wedge and mixed veg	Crusty bread with unsalted butter and some blueberries
Thursday	Banana Porridge with hemp seeds	Kidney Bean Burgers	Mango Chicken Curry with rice (page 134)	Thinly sliced carrot sticks and cheese chunks
Friday	Overnight Chia Oats with banana slices	Mango Chicken Curry with crusty bread	Easy Pizza (page 104) topped with cooked ground beef and peppers	Rice cake with thinly spread peanut butter
Saturday	Banana Pancakes (page 120)	Easy Pizza	Boiled egg* with toast soldiers	Rice cake topped with Greek yoghurt

*British Red Lion eggs are safe to eat when softly boiled. If you do not have Red Lion stamped eggs, serve hard-boiled.

**Choose your bread based on what you feel your baby can cope with! Early weaners will likely need something softer, whereas older babies and toddlers will enjoy French stick or tiger bread.

Shopping list

Fruit & Veg
Bananas
Mango (fresh or frozen)
Raspberries
Broccoli
Carrots
Shallots
Tomatoes
Mint

Meat & Fish
Beef mince
Lamb mince
Chicken breast

Spices & Seasoning
Cumin
Smoked paprika
Garam masala
Garlic granules
Onion powder
Baby-friendly/very low-salt chicken or beef stock (I recommend Piccolo baby-friendly or Kallo very low salt)

Dairy & Eggs
Milk
Eggs
Full-fat cream cheese
Cheese
Full-fat Greek yoghurt

Tinned & Condiments
Chopped tomatoes (for curry and chilli)
Tomato purée
Kidney beans (for burgers and chilli)
Cannellini beans
No-salt sweetcorn
Peanut butter
Coconut milk

Grains & Bread
Oats
Plain flour
Self-raising flour
Sliced bread (low-salt and no soya)
Crusty bread**
Pasta
Rice cakes (plain or from baby snacks section)
Chia seeds
Hemp seeds

Prep Notes: these are things you can do in order to prepare for the future meals coming in the week:

Sunday batchcook Lamb Kofta.

Monday batchcook Chilli, 1 portion in fridge, freeze remainder in portions.

Wednesday make enough Kidney Bean Burgers for 2 lunches, make 2 portions of Overnight Chia Oats.

Thursday batchcook Mango Chicken Curry, keep 1 portion in fridge for Friday, freeze the remainder in portions.

Friday make enough pizza for 2 meals.

Saturday batchbook Banana Pancakes for the following week.

Index

Note: page numbers in **bold** refer to illustrations.

Stage 1: Early Days

Stage 2: Starting to Click

Stage 3: Gaining Confidence

Stage 4: The Big 1!

Stage 5: Graduation

About the Author

Sian (pronounced cyan, like the colour) is the mum, content creator and cook behind TikTok's @moonandrue. She creates content around nutritious weaning meals that are simple to make and can be enjoyed by the whole family.

Throughout university, Sian made content on YouTube and loved the buzz around the creative process of shooting and editing videos. But once she graduated, her life moved very much away from the online world – she spent the next 10 years working in education, first as a secondary school English teacher, and then as a primary teacher. Sian finds child development fascinating and loved being able to have a positive impact during those formative years. Another of her great passions is wellbeing and nutrition. She is a big advocate for learning about food from a scientific basis, not for the purpose of stripping joy away from eating (the joy is the best bit!) but in order to understand the benefits and mechanics of a healthy diet. It helps us underpin why we eat something beyond just, 'it tastes good'.

When she had her daughter, Rue, in 2021, Sian naturally carried these passions into their weaning journey, focusing on making meals that were nutritious, but also complemented developing Rue's skills. In May 2022, Sian began sharing some of her recipes and Rue's meals on TikTok. Comments from parents and grandparents who found the videos helpful in building their confidence with weaning gave her a drive to keep going. She even had messages from university students saying they used her recipes because they were straightforward and reminded them to eat their veggies! Sian is now a full-time content creator and writer, and lives with her husband and daughter in Oxfordshire.

Acknowledgements

My opening acknowledgement couldn't be any easier. My darling Rue, the absolute main character of the last few years of my life. Thank you for bringing endless brilliance, trying all of my recipes no matter how experimental... and being brutally honest with your opinion of them. What a special adventure we have been on. The fact that this book exists is a joint achievement and you have brought joy and laughter to every stage of the journey. A huge thanks also to my husband, Alex. As much as I tease you for your love of regimented routine and planning, it turns out your proactive approach is the perfect remedy to my love of procrastination. This book was a big project, but you've kept me moving forward and never shown anything but support and total belief in me.

A special mention to my mum, who always knows the right thing to say. Her encouragement, praise, advice and excitement throughout this process has been the best boost of confidence. And to Robin, Drew, Luca, Jack, Big Jack and my gorgeous nephews, thank you for being the best support network. My family have put up with a lot of random behaviour throughout my years of dabbling in content creation (thinking back to the days when I used to photograph every meal...), but those moments have all resulted in this book, and knowing they are proud means the world.

A special shout out to my wonderful friends, especially Maria and Ria – they are there for me in everything I do and never fail to hype me up when I need it most.

A big thank you to the amazing team at Yellow Kite and Hodder, in particular, Lauren Whelan, Liv Nightingall, Jenny Platt and Janet Aspey, for holding my hand through the process of my first book. And to the incredible design, styling and photography team, Andrew Burton, Lou Kenney, Charlie Phillips and Lucie Stericker. You are all brilliant at what you do and I feel so grateful to have had such amazing people working on this book. To Yinka Thomas, thank you for casting your expert eye over the project and being so generous with your time and support. Special thanks also to my agent, Stevie, whose guidance and advice motivated me to take a leap of faith and give cookbook writing a go!

Finally, I, of course, have to express my gratitude to my online community. I can't thank you enough for your continued support, kindness and enjoyment of my recipes. It goes without saying that this book would not exist if it weren't for the incredible community that we have built, and I will be forever grateful.

I hope you enjoy this book and that it brings you guidance, ideas and reassurance. Most importantly, I hope you and your babies love these recipes and can make use of them through weaning and beyond!

First published in Great Britain in 2024 by Yellow Kite
An imprint of Hodder & Stoughton
An Hachette UK company

The authorised representative in the EEA is Hachette Ireland, 8 Castlecourt
Centre, Dublin 15, D15 XTP3, Ireland (email: info@hbgi.ie)

2

A CIP catalogue record for this title is available from the British Library

Hardback ISBN 978 1 399 72754 9
eBook ISBN 978 1 399 72755 6

Publisher: Lauren Whelan   **Designer:** Lucie Stericker, Studio 7:15
Senior Project Editor: Liv Nightingall   **Photography**: Andrew Burton
Copyeditor: Helena Caldon   **Food Stylist**: Lou Kenney
Nutritionist: Yinka Thomas MSc   **Prop Stylist:** Charlie Phillips
 RNutr., Public Health Nutritionist and   **Production Controller:** Katy Aries
 Lecturer in Nutrition at Middlesex
 University.

Colour origination by Alta Image London

Printed and bound in Italy by Lego SpA

Hodder & Stoughton policy is to use papers that are natural, renewable
and recyclable products and made from wood grown in sustainable forests.
The logging and manufacturing processes are expected to conform to the
environmental regulations of the country of origin.

Yellow Kite
Hodder & Stoughton Ltd
Carmelite House
50 Victoria Embankment
London
EC4Y 0DZ

www.yellowkitebooks.co.uk
www.hodder.co.uk